PLANNING, DESIGNING AND MAKING RAILWAY LAYOUTS IN SMALL SPACES

Richard Bardsley

THE CROWOOD PRESS

First published in 2013 by
The Crowood Press Ltd
Ramsbury, Marlborough
Wiltshire SN8 2HR

enquiries@crowood.com

www.crowood.com

This impression 2020

British Library Cataloguing-in-Publication Data
A catalogue record for this book is available from the British Library.

ISBN 978 1 84797 424 2

Acknowledgements
Writing a book such as this is more fun than hard work but you can't do it without the help of family and friends. I'd like to thank: my wife Sharon Bardsley for encouragement; my father Stuart Bardsley for proofing; Colin Whalley for letting me play in OO gauge rather than my usual N gauge; everyone at *Railway Modeller* magazine and in particular Steve Flint for allowing me to use their top quality photographs; everyone at the Warrington Model Railway Club and in particular Chris Tungate for letting me photograph their layouts; Bob Rowlands, Peter Johnson, Steve Farmer, Trevor Webster and Kevin Player for letting me photograph their layouts; Alex Crawford for photographing his layout for me.

Typeset by Servis Filmsetting Ltd., Stockport, Cheshire
Printed and bound by Parksons Graphics

CONTENTS

INTRODUCTION

Is space the final frontier for the railway modeller? Certainly not! The space available for your model railway is just one of many parameters that define your layout design. This book will show you how to design and plan the rewarding layout that you want, no matter how tightly defined that space parameter might be.

Real railways are big things. Just take a look at a modern railway and see how much room even a country station occupies. Most railways were built when land was cheap and plentiful. There are real examples of restricted railway sites, although they are mostly located in urban environments. Therefore, even modellers with a large loft or basement face compromises over the space available and this will determine their chosen prototype, train lengths and the amount of scenery. Unless you have a lottery win and move to an aircraft hangar, you will always have to make some concessions on space. But having less space than an aircraft hangar is not a problem – it is an opportunity. There is as much reward to be had in the challenge of working within the space available.

It only requires a surprisingly small amount of space to build a realistic and interesting model railway.

Real railways need big spaces. This five-car Voyager set looks lost at Winwick Junction near Warrington as it progresses from four lines to three amidst the infrastructure of overhead wires and masts. Surrounding fields and a genuinely cloudless sky contribute to a feeling of spaciousness.

You may have to find a little more ingenuity to get the maximum out of the space you have, yet the extra challenge makes it all the more fun.

Most of us have to share our living space with other people and other things and these can reduce a promising-sized space into a smaller one. This is not an insurmountable obstacle; you just have to design into the space and work around it, or even complement everything that surrounds you. Consider a layout that can be 'hidden' in a bookcase, or be the focal point of a room inside a coffee table, or live on a shelf above the furniture of a guest room. You may be able to find space outside the house by using a garden shed or a garage. If all else fails, you can make a layout that is portable – a small layout can be supported on readily available furniture, such as a dining table or kitchen table, or even, believe it or not, an ironing board.

Designing a layout in a small space is still a relevant discipline for modellers with plenty of space, or those who already have a larger layout. It is especially useful if you are a newcomer to the rewarding hobby of model railways. These modellers may want to build a smaller layout for a number of reasons.

Firstly, its relative simplicity means that you will not be overwhelmed by taking on a project that is too big, which may have the worst possible outcome, that you become disheartened and lose interest. A 'quick' layout will bring quick results. Secondly, in the unlikely event that one aspect does not quite go according to plan, you will not have wasted too much money, time and effort. In such a case, you can consider scrapping the layout and starting again in the sure knowledge that the next one will be better, as you will have learnt so much from the first one.

If you believe that you have not got room for a model railway, then think again. Do not think of space as an obstacle – it's only a boundary. You will only ever be limited by the boundaries of ingenuity and imagination, never by space. The aim of this book is to show that you can achieve more with less space. It contains design theory and practical advice, but the main themes are ideas and inspiration. So no matter what area is available to you, there is always a way to design, plan and then make a model railway that you will find challenging, satisfying and, above all, fun.

CHAPTER ONE

POTENTIAL SPACES

No matter how much time you spend thinking about your dream layout, the first practical task of turning that dream into reality is to find a place in which to put it. Planning a model railway involves lots of decisions. What prototype trains will you model? What scale will you choose? Is the scenery going to be urban or rural? You can think about these questions; in fact, you need to think about them because you need to have a clear direction before you set off on construction. Yet the one thing that will literally define the boundaries of your project is the space that it will occupy.

Many houses have a spare room, yet even if you cannot have exclusive rights to all of the room, there are lots of ways to allow your layout to share the space. There are many ways to integrate a layout into the space in a room by using furniture or shelves. Alternatively, you may have more room outside the house than inside – check out the garage or a garden shed. If none of these avenues is possible for a permanent site, there will still be somewhere in the house that can offer a temporary home for your layout, even if you have to make it portable to pack away at the end of the day.

The bigger the space available, the more opportunity there will be for developing your model railway. Yet for many reasons, and in reality for most of us, a large space is not available. Fear not, for there is always somewhere that you can put a model railway layout. If your only previous experience of a model railway was the train set of your youth that was nailed to a piece of chipboard in the corner of your bedroom, be assured that ideas and thinking have come a long way indeed.

ROOM-SIZED SPACES

A dedicated room for your model railway layout is possibly the ultimate luxury for the railway modeller. You may wonder how an entire room (which poten-

tially offers a sizeable space) comes to be included in a book on designing a layout in limited spaces. However, it is assumed that a small bedroom, a garden shed or a garage are the largest of the small spaces to be considered in this book. The scale of the layout relates to space. If you tried to put an O gauge layout into a garden shed, you would find it to be a tight squeeze. And a large space may need to be shared with another household function – for example, you may want also to be able to put a car into the garage, or be able to lodge a guest in the spare bedroom.

SHEDS

The garden shed is considered by many to be the last bastion of male sanctuary – so how appropriate to consider it as a home for a model railway. If you cannot extend your house, then the garden shed offers a fairly low-cost alternative. Sheds come in many shapes and sizes and, therefore, many prices, though, as with everything, you get what you pay for. At the top end you can now purchase an expensive 'outside office' that looks more like a miniature house than a shed. Even traditional wooden sheds can be purchased in quite large sizes. However, for the purposes of this book we shall look at what can be achieved with a traditional garden shed, a simple wooden structure with the modest 6ft × 8ft (1.8m × 2.4m) footprint. Do not be tempted to share the shed with the lawnmower. It will either get in your way, or you will have to move it every time you want to use the model railway. Gardens are all about soil, which is not good for the model railway environment.

Do think carefully about where you might put a shed. If you have a large garden, obviously a small shed is not going to take much off it. If you put the shed too close to the house, you may obscure the garden view, but on the other hand if it's placed at the bottom of the garden there is the risk of a long, cold trek from the house in the dark depths of a British winter (which is often little different from the British summer). While most local authorities do not require planning permission to erect a shed, it might be worth double-checking to be sure and always consult your neighbours. Finally, allow space around the shed for maintenance and repair; do not be tempted to cram it into a corner where you cannot get round for the sake of having a slightly smaller shed.

Some people are disinclined towards the simple timber shed as mixing softwood and British weather is not seen as such a good idea. Choose shiplap cladding (smooth planed and fully interlocking tongued and grooved) to ensure that rainwater drains quickly. Paint your shed with a good quality wood stain (not paint) every year. Non-ferrous hinges are a good investment and make sure that you oil them regularly.

With the requirement to power lights and possibly heaters as well as your model railway, it is important to get the electrical supply safely to the shed. Regulations usually specify that cables should be buried to a safe depth and be of the correct type. Once the supply is in the shed, all electrical work should be carried out to the recommended current practice – sockets and light fittings should be safely installed, with no wires left exposed. As always, the simple advice is that if you are unsure about any aspects of mains electrical wiring, employ a qualified electrician.

Do install ample security, as garden sheds are seen as an easy target by burglars. An alarm and some security lighting are wise investments, as well as a better lock than a simple padlock. As even a modest locomotive collection can be worth a lot of money, consider keeping it in simple rolling-stock storage cases, which can be stored in the house and easily transferred out to the shed for operating sessions. Check your insurance policy as well, since these can be a bit hazy about what is covered in garden sheds. If the policy is not satisfactory, you can get specialist model railway insurance cover for sheds and outbuildings such as garages that is not too expensive.

What may put you off a shed is the potential for wide temperature variations, particularly the cold in winter. However, sheds can be insulated easily and cheaply. Do not use polystyrene sheets, as these are an additional fire hazard in a wooden building and they do not mix well with electrical cabling (they can react together, causing the plastic covering of the wire to fail). Rolls of loft insulation (especially with the silver foil backing) are suitable and easy to install between the framing of the shed. Cross-battens can then be used to retain the insulation; they also form a frame to support your chosen facing for the inside of the shed. The greatest heat loss occurs through windows, door, roof and floor. The roof and door can be treated in the same manner as the walls, while windows can be double-glazed, or, at the least, secondary glazed. The floor is the worst offender for heat loss, since although heat rises, so does dampness. As a minimum, the shed foundation should be flagged and the shed raised above ground level on beams. Most shed floors are just a single layer of wood. Lay insulation or carpet underlay on the floor, then add a plywood layer on top.

Bear in mind that insulating the walls, floor and roof will reduce the nominal sizes inside a shed. If you plan a layout to use a 6ft × 8ft shed, you will not get exactly those internal dimensions. If you are planning your layout before the purchase and fitting out of a shed, allow for these slightly reduced internal dimensions. You can carry on planning, but the best advice is not to cut any wood for baseboards until the shed is finished and the internal dimensions can be accurately measured. Most sheds will have the door in the middle of one of the gable ends, though, unlike rooms in a house, the door opens outwards, which saves having to allow for the door swinging into a room.

A 6ft × 8ft shed is an ideal size, as it allows virtually any type of model railway to be built within, certainly in OO gauge and N gauge. The 18in (0.45m) minimum radius in OO gauge easily accommodates a half-circle from one side of the shed to the other. By fitting a lift-out section in front of the door, it is possible to have a continuous running oval layout, allowing you to just sit and enjoy the trains rolling by.

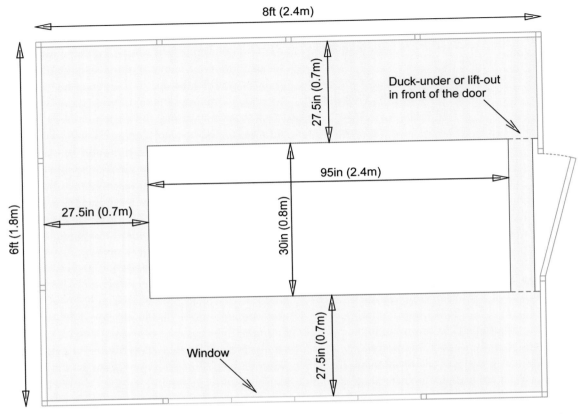

8ft (2.4m)

27.5in (0.7m)

Duck-under or lift-out
in front of the door

95in (2.4m)

6ft (1.8m)

27.5in (0.7m)

30in (0.8m)

27.5in (0.7m)

Window

A typical 6ft × 8ft shed offers just enough space for all the typical layout shapes in the most popular scales.

Carefully consider how deep your baseboards will be. The 'bit in the middle' is referred to as the 'aisle' and there needs to be enough space in the aisle so that you can sit comfortably in the middle of the layout. If the interior width of the shed is just less than 6ft (1.8m) and the baseboard depth on each side is 2ft (0.6m), this leaves less than 2ft (0.6m) in the aisle.

The common 'fiddle yard at the back' type of layout is easily accommodated using one side of the shed. The depth required for the fiddle yard will likely be less than the scenic section. This gives the opportunity to offset the baseboard depths relative to the door, deeper on the scenic side to maximize the scenic potential and narrower on the fiddle yard side. The deeper baseboard will overhang the door opening – you can choose either to squeeze past it, or provide a slight cutaway by the door to make entering and exiting the shed easier.

The larger O gauge is likely to be harder to fit into a shed, since the radii will require more than the 6ft (1.8m) width to complete a half-circle. A modest shunting layout or motive power depot could fit on the 8ft (2.4m) length, possibly with another layout on the other side. These could be separate projects, or joined by the use of cassettes (*see* Chapter 2) to pass stock from one side to the other.

GARAGES

If the garden shed is declining as the natural habitat of the male of the species, the garage is probably taking over. Just over half of the homes in the United Kingdom have a garage, yet it is estimated that only a quarter of these actually contain a car. For many, the garage is simply a black hole to absorb all the junk that modern life accumulates. Modern houses tend to have integral garages accessible from within

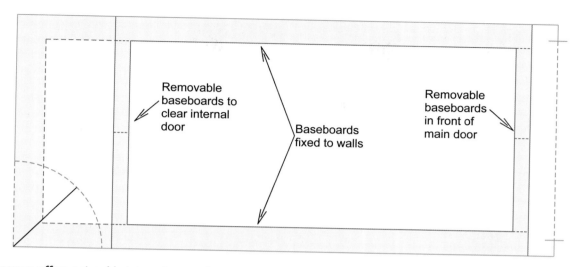

A garage offers a sizeable internal space; however, if it has to be shared with a car the space will be long but without much depth. Removable baseboards in front of the main door will be necessary so as to allow access for a car. Removable baseboards at the back of the garage may also be needed if there is an internal door; with no internal door, the baseboards can go all the way round in a U-shape.

the house, while older properties have standalone garages often of the concrete or asbestos type. More often than not, integral garages have been converted into another room within the house.

Unlike sheds, garages are broadly similar in size. You can expect a garage to be approximately 8ft (2.4m) wide and 18ft (5.5m) long. This is twice as big as the typical 6ft × 8ft (1.8m × 2.4m) shed. Many of the comments about sheds apply equally to garages in respect of insulation, electrical supply and security. All garages are likely to be more weather-resistant; however, even modern integral garages are unlikely to have cavity walls and be plastered. The biggest challenge to temperature will be the large door on the front.

If you only have to share the garage with some paint tins and a lawnmower, there will be a reasonable space left over in which to build a layout. The suggestions for baseboards outlined for sheds apply equally well to the virtually identical footprint of the average garage. One extra consideration might be a side door into the garage as well as the main door, or a door through to the house in an integral garage. If the main door of the garage is still to be used, this means that there has to be a break in the base-

boards to accommodate this door. In a standalone garage, the side door may well open outwards like a shed, but with integral garages the door will most likely open into the garage. If the latter is the case, then a lift-up section can be used to bridge the door opening. It is still possible to use the main door and have a layout in front of it. The layout can be made permanent along the side walls and portable in front of the main door.

This leads on to design considerations in case you actually want to use the garage to store a car. With the car outside the garage, portable sections can be erected in front of the main door for the duration of an operating session. At the end of the session, the portable boards can be taken down and stored out of the way under the main layout. Inevitably, this does not leave much depth for your baseboards. If you want to sit down during operation, it may prove necessary to compromise by having fairly narrow baseboards. If the wing mirrors on your car are the type that fold back, you may gain another couple of inches.

If you do not mind standing up while you operate your layout, you can raise the baseboard height above the normal 'tabletop' height. This may allow you to gain another couple of inches of width. Some modellers actually prefer a more elevated baseboard height as it allows them to get down to eye level with the layout rather than the traditional 'helicopter view' of tabletop height. Another advantage of a higher baseboard is that it increases the storage under the layout. It's not ideal to be storing things (especially heavy and bulky items) above your layout – they only have to be dropped once to do a lot of damage to your layout.

It is easy to measure your garage, but it is also well worth consulting the car manufacturer's brochure to find the exact dimensions of your car. Also, allow for room to open the car door once it is inside the garage, unless you want to end up having to clamber out of the window. When you come to change your car, check the car's dimensions before you buy – remember that the trend is towards larger cars and even if purchasing the same make and model, a mid-term cosmetic facelift may have added an inch here and there.

Most people drive into a garage, rather than reversing in. Therefore, it is likely that you will have to have a narrower baseboard on the right-hand side (as you look in from the main door). As with the shed designs, place a fiddle yard on this side as that is usually narrower than the scenic baseboards.

Those big front garage doors, especially the older 'up and over' type, are likely to let a lot of heat out of the garage around the door frame. Another associated issue is that they can let in a lot of dust and damp, especially when it's windy. Therefore, you may wish to consider a protective cover for your layout when it is not in use. This can be nothing more than a sheet of lightweight polythene; 'wheelie bin' bags are ideal for this. If you use a heavier polythene, be careful not to damage any fragile items such as trees. The next step up in covers would be to make a simple wooden frame to support the polythene sheet. If you have a plywood or MDF back scene at the rear of the layout, it can rest on that. At the front, you can make hinged flaps that fold down while operating the layout – these are a good idea anyway as they will help to avoid damage to the layout when you are doing other things.

Despite these suggestions for mutual coexistence within a garage between a car, a model railway layout and general household junk, you may still find that you cannot get it all to fit. The final option is just to use the space to erect a completely portable layout when the car is outside, though you may find that this limits you to the warmer months of the year. However, you can always spend the long winter months at the kitchen table making some new models and rolling stock.

THE SPARE BEDROOM

We now move into the house and consider the spare bedroom, sometimes called the box room. Most houses average three bedrooms and there's a good chance that the third (and always the smallest) of these will be available. If you are an 'empty nester' with the kids grown up and moved away, this room is quite likely to be spare. More so than sheds and garages, the spare room can be any shape or size. It may be square or rectangular, or even L-shaped due to some peculiar architectural layout of the house. Some spare rooms are so small that you wonder the architect ever thought to get a bed in at all. You may also have to contend with an airing cupboard, which possibly houses a water storage tank and maybe even the heater for it. Another common feature that bites a chunk off the room is an angled bottom to the wall to accommodate the stairs. These 'features' will interrupt the simple rectangular structure of a room such that you have to design around them.

On the assumption that the spare bedroom becomes a dedicated model railway room, there is a temptation to build the baseboards with a degree of permanency. However, even permanent baseboards should be made to be portable. Consider that you may move house – while your next model railway room may not be exactly the same size as the current one, you will want to take your layout with you, with a minimum of disassembly difficulty. If you are not moving house, it still pays to make a permanent layout portable. There can be all sorts of wiring and plumbing under the floorboards that may need to be accessed one day.

Even if the room has just four right-angled corners and no airing cupboard, there is a good chance that you may have to share the room with

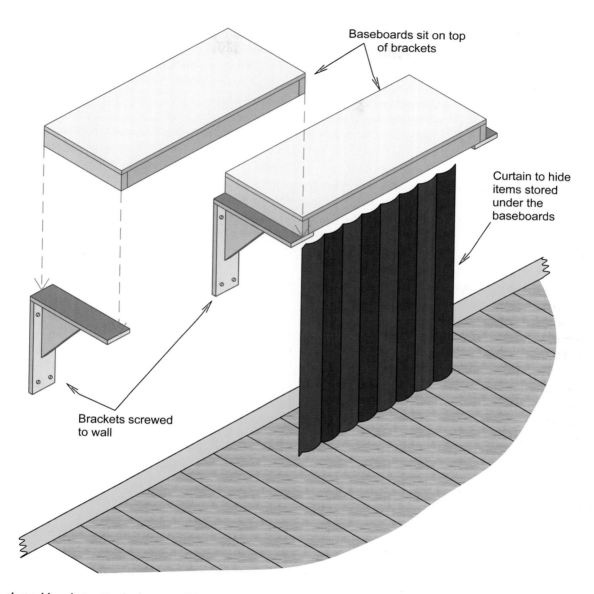

Baseboards sit on top
of brackets

Curtain to hide
items stored
under the
baseboards

Brackets screwed
to wall

L-shaped brackets attached to a wall in a spare room allow baseboards to be supported without cluttering the floor with trestles and legs. Anything from boxes to a bed can be stored underneath, while a simple curtain hung from the baseboard gives a very neat and tidy finish.

some furniture. There may be a wardrobe in the spare bedroom. Like the airing cupboard, you will have to work your design around it. In fact, it may be that the spare bedroom is also a guest bedroom. In this case, the whole room needs to be designed with a dual purpose in mind, though never the same function at the same time. This can be achieved with

a mix of permanent baseboards and semi-portable baseboards, the latter being easily taken down and stored under the permanent baseboards (and when I say 'permanent', bear in mind my earlier comments about 'portable permanency').

The L-bracket system of supporting a layout allows for a lot of flexible storage under a layout.

While the fixing of L-brackets to the wall is a very permanent solution indeed, the baseboards still just rest on top, which makes them easily removed if required. It is possible to store a single bed (with a modest headboard) on its side under an L-bracket-supported baseboard. The bed can be hidden by curtains when the room is being used for a model railway. When it is required as a bedroom, the bed and the fiddle yard can swap places. Using fold-up flaps and covers for the main baseboard will both hide and protect the layout when not in use. By using wooden covers instead of polythene supported by a wooden frame, you can quickly make your layout look like just another piece of furniture. By hiding your layout, your guests will feel much more comfortable in the room than if they were sharing it with a model railway. Unless the guest is a fellow railway modeller, they might possibly consider you to be less eccentric.

Like the garage, there's a good chance that the spare bedroom is also a junk room. However, by using L-brackets, or making shelving or cupboards under the layout, you will be able to neatly hide all that junk away. So if the lady of the house needs any convincing about using the spare bedroom as a model railway room, the winning argument will be that it will look a lot tidier than it does now. You may even have some storage left over for railway-related books, magazines and all that spare rolling stock that won't fit on the layout in one go. If you build your layout in this way, do remember not to prevent some level of access to the underside of the baseboard without having to disassemble half the room to get at it. There is always a chance that a turnout motor under the layout may fail, or a wire may come loose, and you need to be able to get at it to make a repair.

If your room is free of awkward shapes created by airing cupboards and wardrobes, your next biggest headache is likely to be the door into the room. Doors usually open into a room to swing away from the nearest wall, but this is not always the case. It is a fairly simple exercise to hang a door on the opposite side of the frame. Altering the door to open outside of the room is a little more involved (and uncon-ventional) as it requires alterations to the door frame itself. You would also have to consider how the opening of the door into a hallway or landing would interfere with the rest of the house and the movement of the people around it.

While a door describes a relatively modest arc into a room, it does still reduce the amount of available floor space for a layout. This becomes ever more pronounced the smaller the room is. Another option is to replace the single door with a bifold door. This will describe approximately half the arc of a normal door. Finally, if you just cannot afford any space to be taken up by the door, consider converting it into a sliding door. Door runner kits are widely available and they are quite easy to install. You can probably use the existing door as well. Be careful to check that the wall will adequately support the runner (especially if it is stud and plasterboard construction). Equally, be careful of attaching to the ceiling, as the joists are only meant to support the ceiling itself. Some door runner kits include a floor runner as well as hanging the door from a higher runner, and this should be considered if weight may be an issue. A sliding door will only take a thin slice off one wall and that is easily surrendered. While all of these door alterations are relatively easy to accomplish, if you are in any way unsure, do consult a joiner.

Make a sketch of the room before you do any layout design work to identify all the key dimensions. Do not assume that a room will be perfectly square. There is a good chance that one side may be fractionally longer than the other; after all, houses are not built to engineering tolerances. Add to your sketch all the things that are 'in the way' – windows, doors, cupboards and any furniture that will remain. Finally, note where the power sockets are so that you do not put a baseboard leg in front and can also easily reach them to switch your layout on and off.

A LAYOUT HOIST

Imagine if you could just press a button, you hear the hum of a powerful electric motor and your layout disappears out of the way to leave an empty room. It may sound like the stuff of a 'Wallace & Gromit' film,

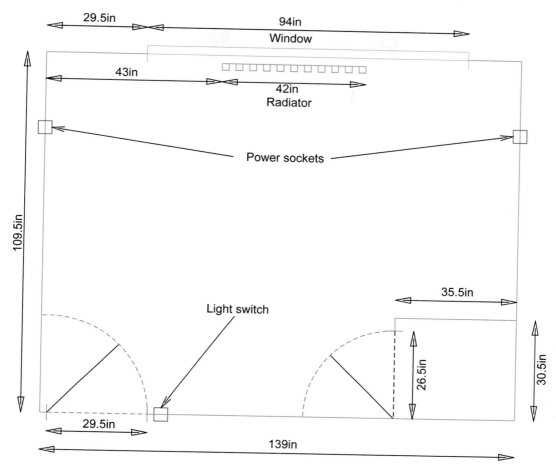

This is a simple plan of my railway room showing all the key features that will influence the shape of potential designs, namely, doors, airing cupboard, window, radiator, sockets and light switch. Inches have been used as the unit of measurement, but you can use whatever you are most comfortable with.

but it is possible and it has been done. There are two types of layout hoist – the lift-up and the fold-up. The former is not very common for the reason that it is not for the faint-hearted, yet the latter offers some practical possibilities. Both are suitable for garages and spare rooms and allow the layout to be quickly moved out of the way to leave the room free for another purpose.

The lift-up layout hoist literally lifts the entire layout up to the ceiling. By suspending the layout at each corner by a wire, you can raise it up to the ceiling and down again. This is a complex solution that requires substantial engineering, not the least

of which is to ensure that the ceiling will take the weight. It is best to fit folding legs under the baseboard in order that when it is down, it does not swing about like a hammock in a storm. Unless you are a competent engineer, a lift-up layout is the sort of thing that is best commissioned.

More practical and easily constructed is the fold-up layout hoist. This pivots one edge of the layout against a wall so that it folds up flat against that wall like a drawbridge. The height of the operating level of the layout will determine its depth, since this is the dimension that must fit under the ceiling when the layout is up. There is less of a limitation on length

Maximum height for scenic items

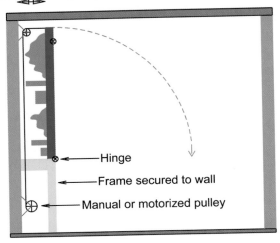

Hinge

Frame secured to wall

Manual or motorized pulley

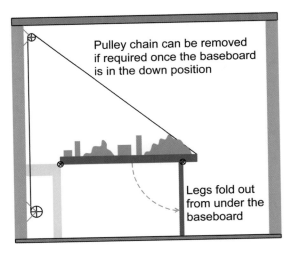

Pulley chain can be removed if required once the baseboard is in the down position

Legs fold out from under the baseboard

A fold-up layout hoist allows a layout to be quickly and easily put away to leave most of the rest of the room space free for other activity. No real engineering skills are needed, just carpentry. The frame and underside of the layout will be visible in the room when it is in the up position but this can always be hidden by a curtain.

though. You could use a pulley system to winch the layout up, but because much of the weight is taken by securing the folding edge to the wall, it is practical to lift up by hand. Make sure you have plenty of secure catches to hold it upright. A couple of security chains are worth considering as well, just in case it was to fall on you. Those chains could be used to hold the layout in the 'out' position, but folding legs are once again a better prospect, especially as they can have adjusters fitted at the bottom. These will ensure that the layout can always be folded down so that it is perfectly level. Remember to set the hinge far enough away from the wall to allow for the tallest scenery and buildings that you are likely to have. Any particularly tall items like factory chimneys can always be removable.

The lift-up layout hoist is probably a bit too 'Heath Robinson' for most modellers, but the fold-up layout hoist could be a practical solution. You can have a reasonable-sized layout erected in the room very quickly with just the rolling stock and a few scenic items to add before you are ready for operation.

FURNITURE LAYOUTS

One of the space challenges faced by the railway modeller is how to integrate the need for space for a layout with the rest of the household's needs for space. If outside space in a garden shed or garage is not available, and there are no bedrooms going spare, you will have to look at sharing an existing space. It may be important to be able to hide the model railway layout when it is not in use, or blend it seamlessly with the room so that it becomes a feature and not an eyesore (if not to you, then to everyone else).

There are two classic examples of layouts that can be built into the furniture. The first is the layout in a bookcase, which offers the potential for a spacious layout discretely tucked into the corner of a room. At the other end of the extreme is the second type, which is the coffee table layout – much smaller in scope yet more of a feature.

BOOKCASE LAYOUTS

The idea of building a layout into a bookcase is not new. If you flick through older railway modelling magazines and books (probably going back forty or

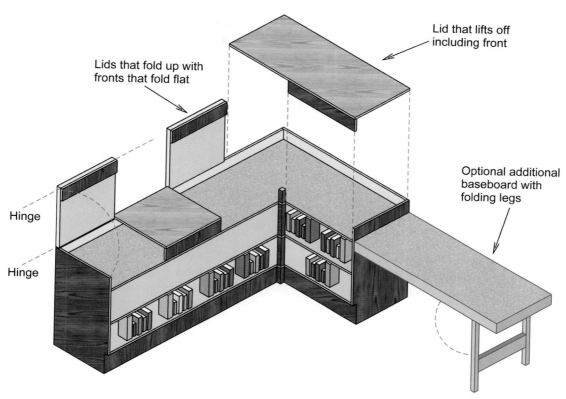

Lid that lifts off including front

Lids that fold up with fronts that fold flat

Optional additional baseboard with folding legs

Hinge

Hinge

A layout in a bookcase easily becomes part of the furniture by virtue of using hinged or removable wooden covers. A temporary baseboard with folding legs can additionally be attached to one or both ends and stored on one of the bookshelves when not in use.

fifty years), you will find numerous examples of the type. If you want to have your layout in a study, a dining room or even a living room, it is an idea that makes a lot of sense. The need for bookcases is still relevant in the modern home. Buying books is more popular than ever, and there are all those CDs and DVDs to store as well.

The length of the bookcase is limited only by what you can (or what you are prepared to) fit into the room. Do not be tempted to make it as long as possible, or you may take over the room, which would defeat the object of sympathetically integrating with the rest of the room's function. Depth is a vital consideration, as most books are not actually very deep. This is less of an issue if you take advantage of the space-saving properties of N gauge, but you may find yourself restricted if you choose OO gauge and a

traditional bookcase depth. So make the bookcase as deep as possible, once again being careful not to dominate the rest of the room. If you go round the corner of the room to utilize two walls, you will need to allow for the minimum radius curve, more of a critical measurement in OO gauge than N gauge. A greater depth of bookcase means you can store even more books under the layout, and to make this easier, consider drawers rather than shelves. You can also store rolling stock and other layout-related things in the drawers.

If you are a dab hand at cabinet making, or at least woodwork, you can build a fully integrated bookcase with layout on top and complete with folding covers as a bespoke solution. For the rest of us, consider using or converting existing furniture. Today, there are many places where you can buy flat-pack furniture of varying sizes and designs. Brochures and websites will provide dimensions, enabling easy calculation of what you can fit in and how you can use it. If you are placing baseboards on top, there are a few things to consider. Make sure that you can finish the baseboards and covers in sympathy with the rest of the furniture – it is no use buying dark oak drawers and using light wood baseboards, as they will clash. Consider staining and polishing the baseboards to match – there is a huge range of such finishes available (test on a spare piece of wood first). The weight of baseboards is important and if your joinery skills tend towards the simpler but heavier softwood and MDF construction, make sure you buy furniture that can take their weight.

Consider a portable baseboard that can be attached to one or both ends of the bookcase for support, with simple folding legs at the other end. This can be used to extend the layout into the room for an operating session and then be stored under the layout (on a shelf) when not in use. This extension board is perhaps best suited to the fiddle yard as it will be flat without scenery and thus a little lighter. There's actually no limit to the number of baseboards that can be piggybacked one on top of the other.

COFFEE TABLE LAYOUTS

Like bookcase layouts, you will find examples of layouts built into tables if you go back in time, but they are a type of layout that seems to have fallen out of favour. To many, they are considered a novelty layout, even a gimmick. But if you are stuck for space, or even if you just want a second layout, why not consider a layout in a coffee table? You can hunt around the furniture brochures once again for a suitable table. Also try looking in second-hand furniture shops – you will find some good solid pre-MDF furniture in these places, which with a little renovation will look as good as new.

The ideal candidate is the sort of table with a glass top and a shelf underneath for magazines. If the glass is frosted or patterned, you can get another piece quite cheaply from a glazier. Do make sure that you get toughened glass and explain what it is to be used

for so that it is safe (if you find a second-hand table, it may be best to replace the glass anyway to be sure). Alternatively, if you do not want the model railway to be a feature on show all the time, use a wooden top that can simply be lifted off for operation. It is quite easy to box in the open sides of the shelf so that the layout can be sealed in. Do not make it too difficult to access the layout if you want a simple 'watch the train go round' design, as if you nudge the table going past, the rolling stock will easily come off.

Coffee table layouts are really the domain of the smaller scales. N gauge is feasible, as you can get a full circle inside a table with a diameter of less than 20in (0.5m). If you want to pack a bit more in, consider Z gauge. There are lots of serious Z gauge modellers, so this is not just the domain of novelty layout builders.

The simple oval layout where the trains just circle round only requires a simple controller to be plugged in. Be careful of trailing wires, as coffee tables tend to be a centrepiece to be walked all the way round. If you want a more challenging layout, perhaps with some shunting, then you will need a control panel, though this can be discretely built into one side of the table. However you choose to operate the layout, you can be sure that a coffee table layout will be an interesting conversation piece when your friends come round.

LAYOUTS IN A DRAWER

This might be thought to be another type of novelty layout, yet what is looked at here is not something tiny tucked away in a kitchen drawer. As a starting point, consider some of the furniture designed for computers. Many of these desks have a wide drawer that supports the keyboard and mouse, and it simply rolls out for use, then back again for storage. Admittedly, you are not going to have a huge layout using this type of furniture as bought, plus things are not really hidden from view when not in use. However, it is the concept that you can potentially make use of.

As with the bookcase layouts, if you are comfortable with joinery, a cabinet can be erected without too much trouble. There is a wide range of drawer

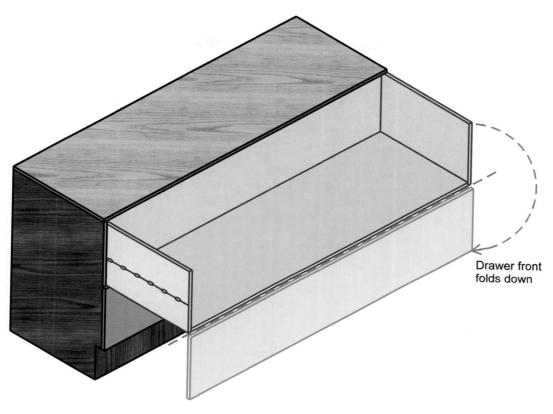

Drawer front
folds down

A simpler though smaller version of the bookcase layout is a layout in a drawer. Just pull out the top drawer, fold down the front and you're ready for operation. Lower drawers can be used for storing rolling stock.

runners available from DIY stores and specialist suppliers. You can get drawer runners that will easily give you a 2ft (0.6m) depth out from the cabinet. A width of up to 5ft (1.5m) is probably the practical limit. As you get towards this width, you may need to add additional runners under the drawer to support it and prevent sagging. The main thing to cater for is the fact that all the weight of the extended drawer is going to be at the top of the cabinet, which is going to make it unstable. To topple over would be a disaster for your layout, but, more importantly, a large piece of heavy furniture falling over could be very dangerous. The simplest prevention would be to fix the cabinet to the wall – many commercially purchased wardrobe and shelving systems do this anyway. Additionally, you may want to consider a leg or two to support the drawer at the front.

If all this seems rather complex, even a tad unstable, consider a simple variation which is akin to the bookcase layout. The drawer is inevitably the same depth as the piece of furniture. Therefore, it stands to reason that if you take the drawer out completely and put it on top of the cabinet, it will occupy virtually the same space. A modest-sized layout using a lightweight baseboard design, say no more than 2ft × 4ft (0.6m × 1.2m), can easily be slid out of the cabinet like a drawer and placed on top. By reversing the drawer when it is out, the inside of the drawer front becomes a back scene for the layout.

You could just about get an oval layout into a drawer space using N gauge; however, it is more likely that you will be building a terminus. A small fiddle yard can be stored in another drawer in the cabinet and attached to the main board on the top

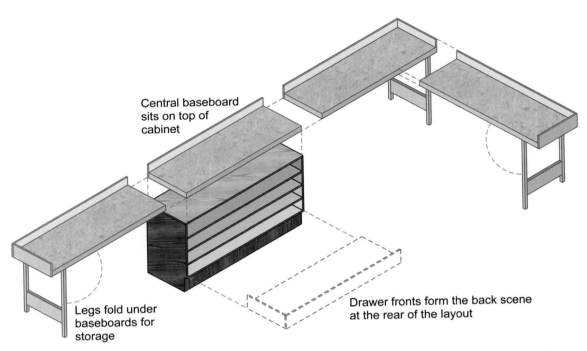

Central baseboard sits on top of cabinet

Legs fold under baseboards for storage

Drawer fronts form the back scene at the rear of the layout

A more sophisticated version of the layout in a drawer enables a larger layout to be built. Each 'drawer' is a baseboard and the drawer front forms the back scene of the layout. The first drawer out forms the baseboard on top of the drawer unit itself. Subsequent drawers use folding legs at one end only to piggyback on to the first baseboard or subsequent baseboards. Baseboards can be attached at right-angles to make the most of the space in a room.

of the cabinet; the outer end of the fiddle yard is easily supported by a folding leg. If you built a longer cabinet, you could store two, possibly three drawers, then connect them together on top of the cabinet. If you are not bothered about hiding the layout completely in the room when it is not in use, then rather than a wooden top to the cabinet, consider glass as you can still see your layout when it is not in use (make sure that you use the correct toughened safety glass).

The cabinet could be designed so that it is really a shelving system, whereby each drawer is a baseboard. To get the layout ready for operation, take the top drawer out and put it atop the cabinet. Take the next drawer out and attach it to the left-hand side, then the next drawer to the right-hand side, and so on. Each baseboard drawer that is attached to the first baseboard can have simple fold-down legs at one end to support it. The number of base-

board drawers you could fit depends on how tall you make the cabinet and the scale you model in – N gauge baseboards will not be as tall as OO gauge ones assuming that the same type of scene is being modelled.

Building your own furniture to hide a layout when it is not in use is not as hard as it sounds. I have built a lot of furniture using no more than MDF sheets and simple wooden framing, and you can get the MDF cut to size at most DIY stores or timber yards. There is a huge range of paint finishes available these days so it is easy to add a sympathetic finish to the rest of your furniture.

You may think that set-up and breakdown times will be prohibitive, but you will be surprised. Once you have practised a few times, you will have the layout up and ready for operation in less than five minutes. It is a potentially ingenious solution to having a layout in your main living space.

The easiest way to support a portable layout is to use fold-up trestles, which you can make yourself or purchase. These trestles were bought from a DIY store as a pair – they are made of lightweight durable plastic, have an integral shelf and fold flat. They are shown supporting a flush-fronted standard-sized internal door that can be used as a simple and cheap ready-made baseboard.

PORTABLE LAYOUTS FOR ANY SPACE

Having looked at room-sized solutions for your layout, such as garden sheds, and spaces within a room, such as a bookcase layout, if none of these provide you with the answer you want, where can you go? The answer is a portable layout. A truly portable layout can be stored in many places that are themselves too small for a permanent layout – under beds, in cupboards, under the stairs and so on. You are effectively making a set of boxes that will store safely and easily and, when joined together, you have a layout. Much of the design relates to where you will then use the layout and how you can support it, such as using nothing more complicated than a table. Generally, you will likely be restricted to narrower end-to-end type layouts, though some designs will support an oval layout in N gauge and smaller.

STANDALONE PORTABLE LAYOUTS

If you go to a model railway exhibition, this principle can be seen in practice on almost every layout. Admittedly, many of the layouts will be quite large, but the idea is just the same – a set of baseboards that can be broken down from the whole, packed into a van, then stored until next time. Most model railway clubs have to adhere to this principle as their clubrooms are not big enough to erect all the layouts permanently. Do not be shy about talking to exhibitors as they love to chat and can explain how they solved the challenge of a portable layout.

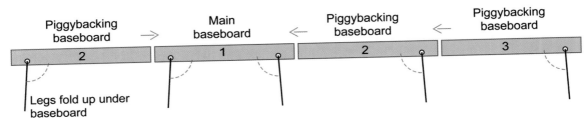

Baseboards with fold-up legs avoid having to store and move separate legs or trestles. One baseboard needs four legs to start you off, but adjacent baseboards only need legs at one end as they can attach directly to the first baseboard, or other baseboards, in a piggyback fashion (the numbers on the baseboards show the order of assembly).

You may have a room in your house in which you can erect a reasonable-sized portable layout. Remember that the bigger you make it, the more baseboards will be needed and the longer it will take to set up and set down. So try not to be too ambitious, or you may end up being put off getting your layout out. All that is required to support a baseboard is a set of trestles that fold flat for storage. In a similar way to the extended bookcase layout, you can make one baseboard with its own set of legs, then piggyback more boards from either or both ends. A modest-sized layout can be easily erected in a room such as a dining room. It can be left up for a few days while you enjoy some operating sessions, then quickly packed away in time to host a dinner party.

TABLETOP LAYOUTS

The dining or kitchen table makes an ideal ready-made base on which to place a portable layout. Many tables, especially dining tables, have an extending portion in the middle to make them bigger, so you can easily accommodate 6ft (1.8m) or more. This is more than enough to make a layout. The table will come with chairs and be just the right height for working at. The narrower baseboard designs leave plenty of space on the table for a control panel, excess stock and a cup of tea. Given the minimum radius of N gauge, it is possible to design a layout with an oval for continuous operation, so you are not just restricted to end-to-end designs.

Do cover your table with a cloth or felt mats before you put a layout on. If you put a scratch on the household's best dining table, you will not be popular. Apart from this, a table makes a superb place to put a portable layout. Boys of all ages have been doing this for decades. A 3mm scale layout would be quite appropriate, as this scale was originally (and sometimes still is) referred to as 'TT' for 'Tabletop'.

FOLD-UP LAYOUTS

This is a variation on the tabletop layout; in fact, you would probably put it on a table rather than trestles. As with some of the other designs in this book, the fold-up layout is not new, yet is not often seen these days. In this design, two baseboards are hinged in the middle, so that for storage, one baseboard folds up over the other, to make a neat box. A simple catch at one end will hold them together. By storing the two halves of the layout facing each other, they are shielded from damage. Simple bolt-on covers for the hinged end and the front (assuming a permanent back scene to the rear) will make things more secure.

You may be thinking that there is a fundamental flaw in this design – if the two baseboards are hinged so that the tops fold into each other, won't all the buildings get squashed? The solution is to raise the hinges, usually on softwood blocks, to a level that clears the scenery on the layout. A few particularly tall features, such as a factory chimney, can be designed to be removable. The blocks to raise the hinges are easily disguised. You can face them with brick or stone sheet to make them into bridge abutments.

A kitchen or dining room table provides a ready-made base on which to put a single baseboard layout and it almost certainly comes with chairs as well for a comfortable operating position. Remember to put a cover over the table to avoid scratching the top surface.

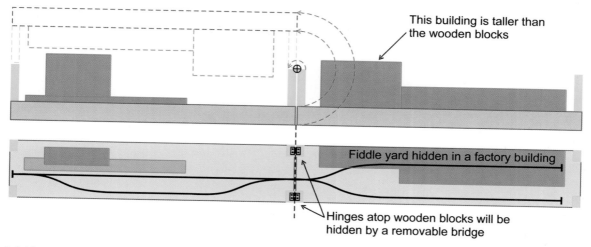

This building is taller than the wooden blocks

Fiddle yard hidden in a factory building

Hinges atop wooden blocks will be hidden by a removable bridge

A fold-up layout consists of two baseboards that are connected by hinges in the middle. This allows one baseboard to fold over the other for storage and portability. They are easy to build, self-contained and ready for action in seconds by unfolding on top of a table. Buildings can be taller than the wooden blocks as long as when it is folded over there is no building on the other half in the corresponding place.

The final touch when the layout is in use is to place a bridge on top so that it covers the hinges. Bridges and tunnels are one of the modeller's favourite tricks to disguise the exit from the fiddle yard. Real railways have hundreds of bridges, so there is no reason why one cannot turn up in the middle of your layout. The bridge does divide the layout into two, but you could put the station on one side and a goods yard or industry on the other.

IRONING-BOARD LAYOUTS

Generally speaking, it is assumed that men and ironing boards will never be seen together. If you do ask your wife where the ironing board is, please do it gently for fear of inducing shock. The ironing board is a design classic and it makes a ready-made stand on which to place a small layout. It is even height-adjustable. A 4ft × 1ft (1.2m × 0.3m) baseboard can be fitted on to an ironing board and this will give you a reasonable shunting-type layout, especially in N gauge. Do make your baseboard as light as possible. An ironing board has very good end-to-end stability, but less so side to side, and if you make it top-heavy, you risk sending your whole layout crashing to the floor. A chair could be used on one side to increase stability, or the layout erected against a wall.

Using an ironing board is a serious proposition. I have seen it used very effectively to support a number of portable layouts and the set-up time is extremely quick, which is one of the prime considerations. Some modellers may dismiss the idea as being in the category of novelty layouts. Yet if you are stuck for space, what better than utilizing household objects that are readily to hand. Unlike a table, it can be erected anywhere in the house, which gives you greater flexibility to work around the rest of the household (unless someone needs to iron a shirt).

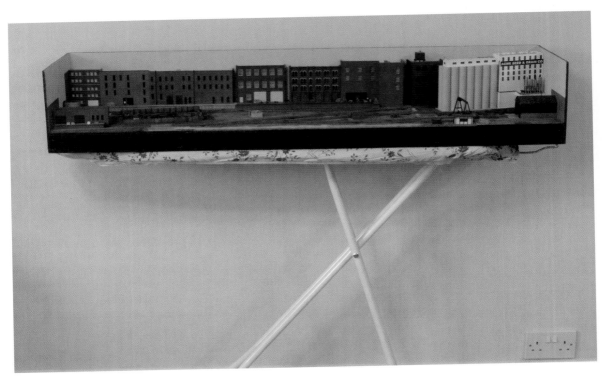

An ironing board makes a surprisingly versatile stand for a small narrow baseboard. It is reasonably sturdy, especially when placed against a wall, is height adjustable, folds flat and has a dual purpose should you feel like doing some ironing ...

CHAPTER TWO

DESIGN PRINCIPLES

All the appliances and conveniences of the modern world are better by design thanks to lots of clever people. Yet you do not need an engineering qualification or a degree in mathematics in order to design your model railway. Design in this context simply means thinking about a few key principles and how they interrelate with each other. For example, the length of the train you can fit into a given space depends on the scale that you choose to work with. In fact, it is largely just a matter of applying good old-fashioned common sense.

A design also means a plan and purpose. You can just let your model railway evolve as you go along. That's fine if that's the way you want to do it and how you enjoy it – railway modelling is one of those hobbies where there is not always a 'right answer' despite what some modellers would tell you. The real reason for introducing a bit of design is to try to avoid mistakes further down the line. You will not eliminate mistakes altogether – we're only human. However, a little design goes a long way, and hopefully this will help you to avoid some of the pitfalls.

Where space is restricted, design is doubly important. As things get smaller, tolerances become more critical. You want to make the most of the space so that every inch counts. This chapter looks at a few sensible design principles that apply to all model railway layouts, but particularly to those situations where space is at a premium.

CONSIDER SCALE

It is an obvious thing to say, so let's say it – choose your scale carefully. Each of the major scales has something going for it, yet each will have its drawbacks. Equally obvious is that the less space you have, the more you will get in that space if you choose a smaller scale. That could be more scenery, more track, or just longer trains. The three major commercial scales are O gauge, OO gauge and N gauge.

There are several other scales, although you may find that you need more experienced modelling skills to exploit them. Rather confusingly, each scale is referred to by its 'gauge', when scale is an actual measurement of its relationship to the prototype.

Starting with the biggest first is O gauge. This is a scale of 7mm to the foot. Although ready-to-run models are becoming increasingly available, it is still largely a kit-builder's scale. While O gauge hardly seems a scale for small spaces, in fact in can be used in a shed or room location. However, you would most likely be limited to an end-to-end type layout, as the radius for an oval in O gauge would be too tight for all but the most generous of rooms. There are some superb O gauge layouts that utilize small spaces. These tend to be shunting-type layouts, so if a few sidings to shuffle wagons about is your thing, give O gauge some serious thought. The larger scale means that a high level of detail can be incorporated into the rolling stock and scenery. If you enjoy that level of fidelity, then this will outweigh the compromise of being able to have less in the available space.

The most popular commercial scale is OO gauge, a scale of 4mm to the foot. It sits pretty much in the middle of the commercially popular scales in terms of size, which helps to explain its popularity. There is a huge range of ready-to-run rolling stock and supporting scenic items available. Modern ready-to-run locos have the fidelity and detail previously only seen in O gauge, yet the scale takes up half the space. You can achieve an oval layout in a room with OO gauge, as the radius required is, of course, much less than O gauge. Of all the scales, it is perhaps the one that offers the fewest compromises, since a high level of detail is possible without taking up too much space.

The smallest commercial scale is N gauge. At 2mm to the foot, this gives you the most in your available space. It has enjoyed a huge resurgence in the last

The smaller the scale, the more can be fitted on to the layout. This is the same 21T 12ft wheelbase mineral wagon in (from back to front) O gauge, OO gauge and N gauge.

ten years, with a massive increase in the range and fidelity of the ready-to-run models available. This gauge allows the most opportunity to exploit scenic potential. Oval layouts are easy, but the option is still there to model an end-to-end layout. If you are really constrained for space, or want a novelty layout such as one in a coffee table, then N gauge means that you are never stuck for space.

At 3mm to the foot, TT gauge (more usually referred to as 3mm scale) is an ideal scale for the modeller with space restrictions. It has all the fidelity and appearance of OO gauge, yet the reduction from 4mm to 3mm gains a lot of precious space, lying as it does exactly halfway between OO gauge and N gauge. It was first marketed as 'TT' with ready-to-run equipment from Tri-ang. It is perhaps a shame that it never really took off as a commercial scale, though modern N gauge now offers all the space

advantages of 'tabletop' or 'TT' capability, but with a level of fidelity that now far exceeds those early Tri-ang models. There is a 3mm Society, which gives good support to modellers, although it is largely a kit and scratch-building scale and thus one for the more experienced modeller.

Finally, there is Z gauge, a scale of 1.4mm to the foot. Remarkably, there are ready-to-run locomotives and coaches available, plus track and scenic accessories, though the prototypes are usually North American or European. Oval layouts are simple to achieve in all but the smallest spaces; however, shunting and end-to-end type layouts would be a challenge to all but the most dexterous.

The simplest way to get more out of your available space is to switch scales – drop from O gauge to OO gauge, or from OO gauge to N gauge. Do not be a slave to your favourite scale if to change it would allow you to exploit your space more fully for the type of model railway that you want.

TRAIN LENGTH

In real life, even a short train is surprisingly long. Railways take up a lot of real estate, but they are mostly long, thin things. A British Railways Mark One coach is 63ft (19.2m) long – that's 5.1in (12.9cm) in N gauge, or 9.9in (25.2cm) in OO gauge. A modest rake of four coaches will be about 3ft (1m) long in OO gauge. In a 6ft × 8ft (1.8m × 2.4m) shed, by the time a locomotive has been added to the front, that's half the space of the main side wall taken up with just one train.

There is an oft referred to principle of train length in relation to layout size, namely, the principle of thirds. This states that a single train should occupy no more than one-third of the visible space on a layout, or a single scene within a layout. The idea behind this principle is that the train then looks to be 'within' the scene and not simply occupying the entire scene. The worst violation of the principle would be where the scene is smaller than the length

of the train, so that it is impossible to see the whole train at any one time. It is an interesting aspiration, but it does not need to be an overriding aim. Anyone who has ever tried to photograph real trains will tell you that there are plenty of situations where you cannot find a vantage point from which it is possible to see the whole train.

A lot depends on what sort of railway you wish to model. If you tend towards the classic branch-line terminus, the trains are short, no more than two coaches in a passenger train and half a dozen wagons in a freight train. This is certainly achievable in most spaces in OO gauge. At the other extreme, if you want to model a full-blown main line with ten-coach express trains, this will not be possible in OO gauge, but it probably will in N gauge. Once again, you need to choose your scale carefully in relation to the type of trains and railway that you want.

If you do want an express train, even in N gauge, be prepared to compromise. A real main-line express may consist of ten coaches – consider pruning this a little while keeping the essence of the train. If the ten coaches were made up of one parcels, three first class, five second class and a dining car, try reducing

Both of these trains are headed by a Prairie tank loco with a guards van on the back. The train at the rear has a pair of each of the three intermediate wagon types. The front train is quite a bit shorter, yet it still captures the feel of the train with one of each wagon type.

it to one parcels, one first class, three second class and a dining car. That is now six coaches in total, a reduction of 40 per cent. However, it keeps the main features of the train (parcels, dining, first and second class). Freight trains can be similarly reduced and this is a little easier. Block trains comprise all the same wagon; for example, a full Merry-Go-Round (MGR) set can be thirty-six wagons. A set of twelve is just one-third of the full length, yet it is still a long train. Mixed freights are easy to reduce. As long as you have a nice variety of wagon types, a short train will look just as good as a long one.

Smaller trains on a smaller layout do not look out of place. The chances are that there will be scenic breaks such as trees, buildings, tunnels and bridges. Deliberately working against the principle of thirds can be to your advantage. If you cannot see the whole train at once, you do not know how long it is.

Therefore, it does not matter if it is shorter than it would be in real life. Think about a greater frequency of trains. Sometimes, real railways split trains into smaller portions for operational reasons such as the length of loops or severe gradients. If you have a good fiddle yard system, for every long train you might have, you can actually store two short trains.

Room-sized layouts offer a degree of freedom in train length. In a reasonable oval layout around a room, reductions in prototype formations of at least 50 per cent will still leave realistic trains. However, what if you have an end-to-end layout on a table-top or a bookcase? The selective reduction of train length still applies, which means that a long express train is probably out of the question. Selecting a pro-totype away from the main line offers the chance to have short trains that are realistic. You do not have to go all the way down to a branch-line terminus;

A greater number of shorter wagons can be fitted into a siding than longer ones. This short siding runs from the toe of the turnout on the left to the trees on the right and will only take three 12ft wheelbase hoppers.

This is the same siding, now with four 10ft wheelbase hoppers. The train length is only slightly longer, yet by having an extra wagon (effectively an increase of one-third), the siding looks more 'busy'. This creates an illusion of having more in less space.

many town or seaside stations offered good train lengths, often in a realistically cramped setting.

If you are building a very small layout, such as a micro-layout, or a small shunting layout, pay particular attention to the length of individual items of rolling stock. If you already own the models, measure their length. Remember to measure all the way over the coupler, since the coupler determines how close a piece of rolling stock gets to the next one. If you do not own the models yet, contact the manufacturer, or ask nicely at your local model shop to see them. There will be varying lengths even to the same type of rolling stock. The wheelbase of a wagon is a good guide. Original wooden-bodied coal wagons had a 9ft (2.7m) wheelbase. This increased to 12ft (3.7m) for steel-bodied opens, a one-third increase in length. Using these lengths as a very rough guide, for every

three of the 12ft wheelbase wagons you can fit four of the 9ft wheelbase wagons. If you model, say, the British Railways period when both types of wagon could be seen together, consider using the four shorter wagons instead of the three longer ones to give a greater visual impact. The train length is the same, yet the extra wagon can fool the eye into thinking that it is longer.

There are other factors on a layout that will determine train length. Platforms need to hold a locomotive and coaches. If the station is a terminus, the train (just the coaches, there is no need to include the locomotive) must be shorter than the run-round loop. The fiddle yard must be able to hold the longest train you will use. All these factors influence the other; none need be longer than any of the others. So if the run-round loop will hold two

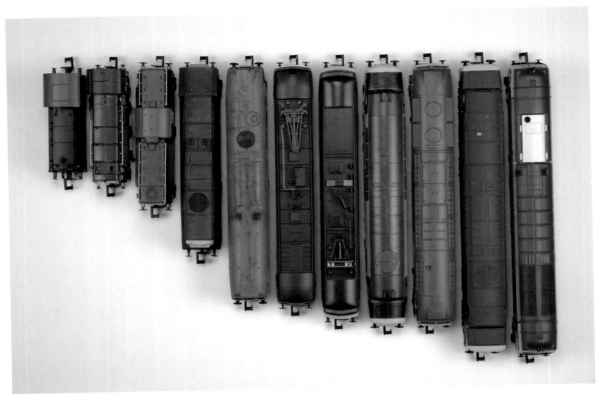

It is important to know how long each item of rolling stock is so as to be able to work out what can be fitted into sidings and loops. Do not measure just the length of the body – note how these N gauge locomotives have been lined up so that the couplings are level at the top. Obviously, there is a huge difference between the Class 04 on the left and the Class 60 on the right; however, differences between Classes 31, 86, 90, 37 and 47 in the middle are more subtle.

coaches, the platform needs to be two coaches plus locomotive in length, as does the fiddle yard. Being able to accommodate four coaches and a locomotive in the fiddle yard would be pointless in this example.

Always take the time to measure your rolling stock before you plan your layout. You only have to measure each type of locomotive, carriage or wagon once. Keep a note, even a simple table of lengths, either multiples of the same or different combinations. Finally, consider drawing the proposed trains on pieces of paper either to actual model size or half size. There is no better way to visualize the end product than having something tangible to play with. This will help you to avoid costly mistakes in the track layout. The last thing that you want to discover

is that your platforms are too short for the trains you want to run.

One final thought on train length is the couplings that are used. Both OO gauge and N gauge use almost exclusively a standard coupling (the 'tension lock' and 'rapido', respectively). They may be pretty ugly but they both serve the purpose of fairly easy coupling and uncoupling, pulling and propelling. It is the latter where the train set origins of these couplers show, as they keep the rolling stock artificially separated to prevent buffer locking. This artificial separation means that rolling stock is much further apart than it should be. On a long train of short wheelbase steam-era wagons, this could mean as much as one extra wagon lost to the additional distance. Buffer-locking occurs (sometimes even with

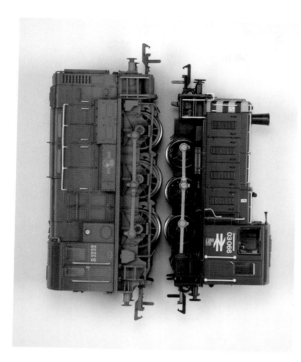

As well as measuring the length over the couplers, measure the wheelbase of locomotives. There is not a huge difference in length between the Class 08 on the left and the Class 03 on the right; however, the latter has a much shorter wheelbase. This means that it will take up less room on the track by turnouts and in fiddle yard solutions such as sector plates.

real trains) on very tight corners, usually on the transition from the straight to the curve – as the wagons enter the curve, the inner radius forces the inner buffers of adjacent wagons together, sometimes enough to cause a derailment. It may also happen with propelling moves. The extra distance of the model couplers prevents the buffers from touching.

There are several alternative couplers available. In O gauge, using realistic three-link couplers is almost standard and is quite possible in OO gauge (although a little fiddly). It is not necessary to convert all your

The couplings used in the smaller scales can take up more room. These two OO gauge wagons are as close as it is possible to get them, yet the buffers are unrealistically too far apart. Using a closer coupling would allow more wagons in the same space; however, the savings are slight and would only be noticeable over a very long rake of wagons.

rolling stock if you use fixed rakes of coaches and wagons. The inner wagons can be converted to a closer coupling, with standard couplers just left on the outer ends of the rake and on locomotives for ease of use. Whatever alternative coupling method you may choose, it will still require a lot of conversion work. Some of these couplers require construction, plus some fiddly adjustment and maintenance to get them to work properly. You have to ask yourself if it is worth the effort for a modest saving in train length, although the aesthetic improvement alone may make it worthwhile.

CURVES

If you are building an end-to-end layout, you might be tempted to skip this section. Read on, however, because there is more to curved track than first meets the eye. If you have a room or a shed, then you will probably be building an oval layout, in which case you need to pay particular attention to the radius of your track at each corner. The first question is – how tight a radius can you have? The answer lies in sectional track (sometimes called 'set track'), which is the track you may have started with in a train set. The track components are made to fixed geometry (as opposed to flexible track, which can be curved to any radius or combination of radii).

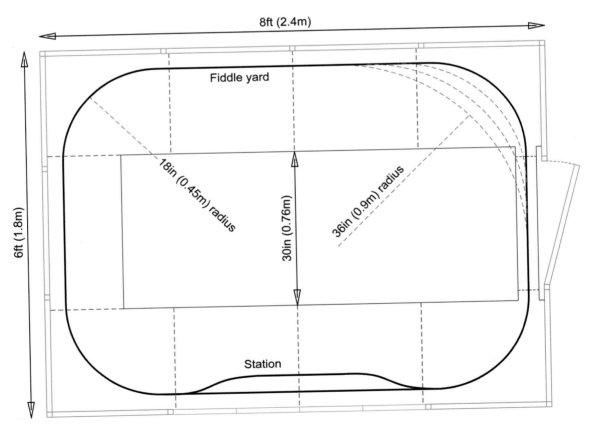

The more generous the curves, the more they will encroach into a room. This simple layout has 18in curves around a typical 6ft × 8ft shed. This is about as tight a radius as you would want to go in OO gauge. Some alternate curves (with dashed lines) are shown top right, in 6in increments up to 36in. However, note how they start to encroach on to the lift-out section in front of the door and into the space available for the fiddle yard.

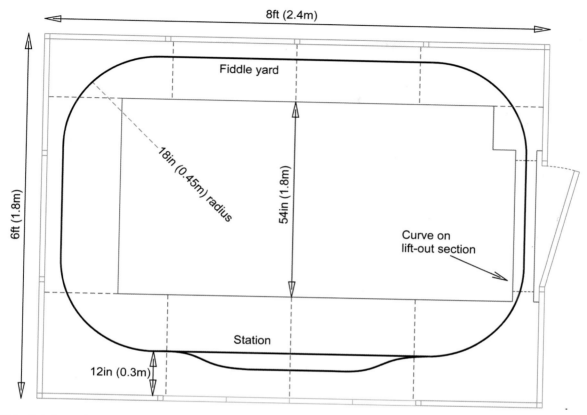

This slightly modified design has retained the 18in radius curves to maximize the length of the station and the fiddle yard. The station has been moved away from the wall; the station baseboards are wider and the ones in the fiddle yard narrower. This is a more typical set-up for a room-sized oval layout, but it does mean that even the 18in radius curves are encroaching on to the lift-out section by the door.

It is not limited to train sets and there are several developed ranges of sectional track offering a range of fixed radii that relate to each other.

Traditionally, the minimum radius in OO gauge is 18in (0.45m), while in N gauge it is 9in (0.23m). Most rolling stock will just about run round these minimum radii in each scale. However, some manufacturers making a modern generation of model locomotives are publishing a minimum radius greater than these traditional values. There is a trade-off between the greater fidelity of these modern models against the 'train set' appearance of very tight curves. Just like real trains, your model trains will generate greater friction on the track as they pass into the curves. Modern locomotive models are powerful and the

rolling stock is very freewheeling, but it is something to be aware of – you do not want to see your train stalling, with wheels spinning, halfway around a curve.

Consider for a moment the 6ft × 8ft (1.8m × 2.4m) shed and assume for simplicity that those are the internal dimensions (as insulation will reduce these nominal measurements). Working in OO gauge, if you have 18in (0.45m) minimum radius corners on an oval design, you need at least 18in of baseboard in each corner for the curve; a larger radius requires a larger baseboard in the corner. It also assumes that the track runs around the very edge of the shed with just 4in (0.1m) of clearance from the walls, which would mean that all your sidings were on the inside

The middle of bogie rolling stock will overhang on the inner face of a curve and this becomes more pronounced the tighter the radius. Hold a pen or pencil to the middle of the longest piece of rolling stock and run it around the curve to mark the minimum level of clearance required for signals and other line-side infrastructure.

of the oval and you had no room for scenery. If you allow 12in (0.3m) clearance on one side (let's say the other is a fiddle yard and thus a narrower baseboard), then you can put the station more into the middle of the scenic section. However, as the curves have moved towards the centre of the room, they may start to encroach on where the door is, or on to what you have allowed for a lift-out section.

The next consideration with tight curves is that they can look unrealistic, although it is only really noticeable with bogie rolling stock. Short wheelbase wagons that are typical of the steam era look fine on a tight corner. The main problem with modern coaches is their length. A British Rail Mark 3 coach is 70ft (21.3m) long – a model of such a vehicle will therefore overhang the inner face of a tight curve

quite considerably. You need to allow plenty of room for this overhang so that it will not foul signals or fences. The classic approach is to hold a pencil in the middle of your longest piece of rolling stock and use it to draw a line that will represent the minimum clearance required.

It is not just the inner face of the curve that needs to be catered for. Some models will stick out at the ends on the outer face of the curve. Long locomotives are prone to this, so allow plenty of clearance on the outer face as well. Short tank engines look fine. There is a relationship between rolling stock and curvature in terms of what looks real and what looks like a toy – it is a matter of proportion. Do not even attempt a platform on a tight corner. By the time you have allowed for the middle of your

Rolling stock (mainly locomotives) can overhang on the outside face of a tight curve. The Class 9F steam loco and Class 40 diesel on the left stick out by an extremely unprototypical distance. Ask yourself whether or not this looks acceptable to you. The shorter Class 04 diesel shunter and 'Jinty' tank engine on the right look much more realistic on exactly the same radius of curve.

longest coach, the passengers will need to be long-jump competitors to reach the doors at the end. The phrase 'mind the gap' has never been more appropriate.

However, even if the unrealistic appearance of a tight curve offends, do not dismiss a design that will make the best use of available space at the cost of tight corners. Quite simply, you can disguise the corners in a number of ways. The most obvious is to bury them in a tunnel. Assuming an 18in (0.45m) radius in OO gauge, you will lose just over 18in at each end. With our 6ft × 8ft (1.8m × 2.4m) shed again, that is 3ft (0.9m) off the 8ft (2.4m) length, leaving 5ft (1.5m) to play with for a station. With a tunnel, you lose the chance to run sidings into the area to the side of the curve. Also, do not put a tunnel mouth at the exact point where the curve

ends and the straight track begins. The principles of overhang explained earlier will still apply, so you may find that coaches and locomotives foul the side of the tunnel mouth.

If you do not want tunnels, there are many other ways to disguise the curve. Consider a cutting, maybe with a bridge or two. As the train moves through this landscape, the scenic features help to distract the eye away from the curve. This is the same trick as described earlier to disguise a reduced train length. In an urban setting, the careful placement of buildings will have the same effect.

If you are an end-to-end layout builder and have read this far, this is the bit for you. As a layout becomes smaller, inevitably the closer the track gets to the baseboard edge. If the track is straight and parallel with the edge of the baseboard, it only

If tight curves look too tight but are essential to your design, consider disguising them or hiding them altogether. This locomotive and three coaches will occupy a quarter-circle of the curves at the end of the layout, but the interaction with the overbridge helps to distract the eye from this.

serves to enforce the artificial nature of the scene portrayed. I call this 'parallel baseboard syndrome', because the eye is good at recognizing perfect geometric shapes. If you present it with a layout that is uniformly parallel, you will see it as a construction and not a realistic representation of another time and place.

It is very simple to break up this pattern recognition in the brain. If you want a straight platform, try placing the track at a diagonal across the baseboard. If the track is running through countryside, introduce a few gentle reverse curves – these create a subtle S-shape from one end of the baseboard to the other. Avoid placing many sidings parallel to each other – try splaying them out like the fingers on a hand. At least curve the outer siding in a goods yard – consider putting the coal staithes or cattle dock between those outer two sidings to give the

impression of a large yard. Finally, if you are confident with your carpentry, build a curved baseboard to match the track instead of a rectangular one. Real railways like straight lines – they are easier to build and maintain. As modellers, we can take the opposite approach – a few curves will actually make your layout look much more realistic.

The gap between two railway lines is referred to as 'the four foot'. Proprietary track systems tend to increase this slightly to make sure that there is a generous gap between the tracks to avoid models that are slightly 'out of gauge' fouling each other. This becomes more acute as the lines move into the curve. The middle section of a bogie coach on the outer line of the curve will overhang the four foot, while the front of a large steam loco on the inner line will hang into the four foot. The result is the potential for a collision. Therefore, bear in mind

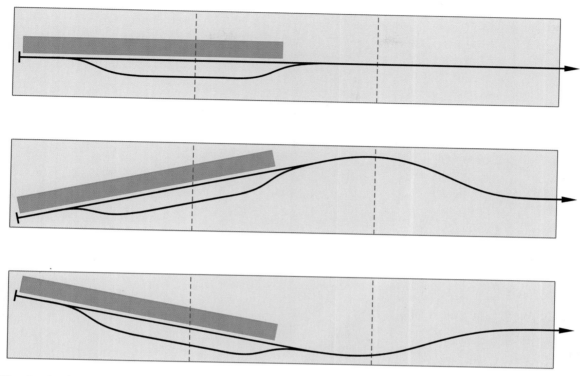

The simple plan at the top over three baseboards is typical of a terminus layout with a station on the left and an approach on the right. All the track is parallel with the front and rear baseboard edges – it looks regimented and small. The middle and lower plan introduce some curvature to the approach, which allows the station to be set at an angle. These plans make the layout appear to be bigger and certainly more interesting.

any overhangs from rolling stock. The solution is to increase the gap between the lines as they go around the corner to allow a greater clearance.

TURNOUT LENGTH

Real railways build their turnouts precisely to fit a specific location. You can build your own turnouts as well, though this is something for the more experienced modeller. Thankfully, the model track manufacturers produce a range of turnouts that are integrated into the geometry of curved sectional track. Every turnout has at least one curve to it in order to diverge the track away in a different direction. Just like the sectional track, some turnouts have a pretty tight radius. The advice about checking the overhang of your longest rolling stock on curves applies equally to the curves in turnouts.

Like curves, the greater the radius of a turnout, the more realistic it will be. This is less obvious in goods yards when shunting at a slow speed. However, consider an express train changing from the fast line to the slow line at speed – using sectional track tight-radius turnouts, the train will wiggle one way, then the other, and might even derail. The larger radius of so-called 'express turnouts' will make the train snake smoothly from one track to the other.

An interesting trade-off of the differing radii of turnouts is their length. It is a simple matter of geometry that the turnout has to be longer to accommodate the bigger radius. For example, a Peco OO gauge code 100 'small radius' turnout is 7.3in (185mm) long. The 'medium radius' turnout is 8.6in (219mm). A difference of 1.3in (34mm) may not sound much. Yet with one turnout at each end of a run-round loop, that is 2.6in (68mm). Over a fan

Double tracks may require additional clearance between the tracks to allow for the inwards overhang of rolling stock on the outer track and the outwards overhang on the inner track. The ends of the white-roofed coaches appear to touch the middles of the grey-roofed ones on the outer track, but there is actually just enough room to avoid a collision.

of sidings it will be more. In relation to train length, it could be the difference between having an extra wagon or not. On a room-sized layout, such modest savings are useful but not essential. For the small layout builder, particularly micro-layouts, every little bit counts.

There are several specialist turnouts that will save you even more space. The most complex turnouts are called slips, either a double slip or a single slip. These are the equivalent of a crossover and either four turnouts (for the double slip), or two turnouts

(for the single slip). That's a lot of turnouts compressed into a small space. They would really only be found in stations and at junctions, rarely in goods yards. As they are complex, that means they are expensive, both to build and to maintain (and similarly, the ready-made model varieties are not cheap either). For this reason, real railways avoid them. However, there is no doubting their huge space-saving capabilities, so if you want to use one in a goods yard, then do so. If it is the difference between your layout design working or not working, a little

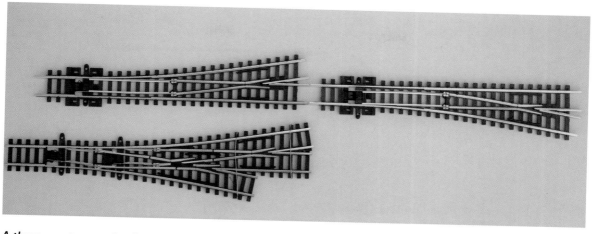

A three-way turnout is a huge space saver. All three of these Peco N gauge turnouts use the same radius of 18in (0.46m), yet using the three-way turnout saves about half the space of the two individual turnouts. This also means that the sidings can be longer.

bit of licence with the use of a slip away from the main line is entirely justified.

The final type of specialist turnout is the three-way turnout. This is basically a left-hand turnout and a right-hand turnout combined into one. Once again, the compact nature of these turnouts makes them more complex, but nowhere near so as the slips. Therefore, they often were (and still are) found in yards on real railways. With the ability to save at least half the required turnout space to get three sidings, rather than use two turnouts, consider using a three-way turnout instead.

For the ultimate in saving the length of a turnout, do not use a turnout at all. The function of a turnout is to swap a train from one track to another. There are other ways to achieve this, such as using traversers and sector plates. As these are fiddle yard solutions, that is where these turnout substitutes will be situated, since they are not really prototypical (though there are actually one or two examples of real railway situations where traversers and sector plates were used to save space). Traversers and sector plates will generally only be long enough to hold a locomotive and possibly one or two wagons, so they are not the answer for a whole train (unless as part of the wider fiddle yard solution). They basically combine the turnout and the headshunt

into one, which reduces the amount of space that would otherwise be needed.

FIDDLE YARDS

The fiddle yard represents the rest of the world, a world outside of what you have modelled on your baseboards. To be more precise, it represents the rest of the railway network far and near. If your layout set in Cornwall receives a van load of whisky from the Scottish highlands, it may only have travelled a few inches from the fiddle yard, but, in the imagination, it has come hundreds of miles via several marshalling yards and numerous freight trains. Fiddle yards are important to most layouts, but they are vital to layouts in a small space. We all accumulate over time far more rolling stock than we can fit on to a layout in one go. The fiddle yard is a means of rotating stock, even getting it on and off the layout. It is a way of feeding a procession of trains on to (or through) a layout, rather than watching the same train go past as you would with a train set. Fiddle yards themselves can take up masses of space, which is great if you have it to spare. However, they come in several different types, each with their own advantages.

With an oval layout that has a fiddle yard on one side and a station on the other, you do not have to

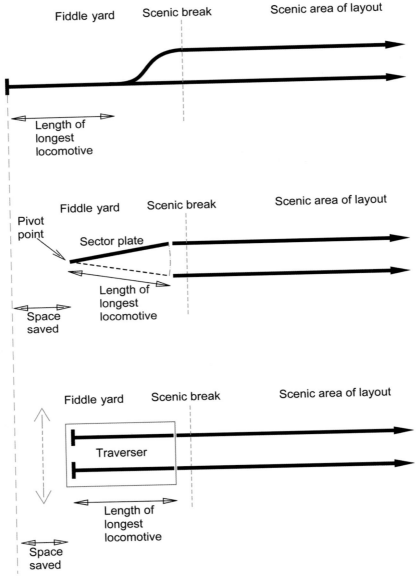

Instead of the turnout arrangement in the top diagram to move between two tracks off-scene, a small amount of space can be saved by using a sector plate (shown in the middle diagram), or a traverser.

run the same train around and around for hours on end. You can run a train clockwise, then a different train anticlockwise. With a number of sidings in the fiddle yard, a whole sequence of trains can be run with a reasonable time between repeats. This gives a more realistic feel to the station, as it looks like it really is somewhere between two points with a flow of traffic passing through. This can be seen in action at model railway exhibitions; the oval layouts that employ this technique are more entertaining.

Alternative names for fiddle yards are 'staging' (an American term), 'storage tracks', or 'hidden tracks'; each term is suitably descriptive. There is a subtle difference between fiddle yards and storage tracks, even though we generically apply the term 'fiddle yard' to anything that is not part of the main layout. We need to distinguish between an area designed simply to hold trains (a sequence of trains made up of a fixed set of rolling stock to run around a usually oval layout) and a place to really 'fiddle' with the rolling stock — turning trains for terminus layouts, changing the make-up of goods trains, swapping locomotives for trains and so on. The former needs plenty of tracks, but those tracks can be squashed together as there is no need for 'fiddling room'. The latter needs lots of room for fingers and hands to get in and handle the items of rolling stock.

If you are exhibiting a layout, all the swapping of trains should be done away from the public gaze of the layout, otherwise the 'big hand in the sky' will shatter the illusion you are working so hard to create. At home, while you may not have an audience, you are still creating an illusion of reality, so there is a psychological advantage to doing all your 'fiddling' in a defined area away from the layout —

it helps to maintain the illusion that the train now arriving has actually come from far, far away.

SIMPLE ONE-TRACK FIDDLE YARD

The simplest fiddle yard can be nothing more than a single piece of track that is off-stage from the rest of the layout. This does require a lot of handling of rolling stock, for example to swap the locomotive from one end of a passenger train to another. The more you handle your models, the more chance there is of dropping or damaging one. Even the natural oils on the skin of your fingers can damage paint finishes over time. The single track is perhaps best for shunting layouts where you are usually swapping short freight trains or just a few wagons — in other words, a limited number of very short trains. It will take up hardly any space, so it is ideal to place at the rear of a layout hidden by a scenic portion in front, as long as the back of the layout is accessible. This maximizes the amount of the baseboard that you can use for layout, with the bare minimum as fiddle yard.

A fiddle yard need be no more than a single siding of track, as illustrated here with Peter Johnston's N gauge layout, 'Rosneath'. It is simple and compact, although it does require more handling of rolling stock and 'fiddling'. Note also the toe end of a turnout on the far right, which means that the fiddle yard needs to be kept clear to act as a headshunt for some of the moves on the layout.

A ladder fiddle yard is so-called because the parallel sidings look like the rungs of a ladder. These can have through tracks for oval-type layouts, as at the top, or dead-end tracks for terminus layouts, as at the bottom. Short sidings can also be included off the loops, as at the top right.

LADDER FIDDLE YARD

The next logical step from the single track is a set of sidings reached by turnouts, often called a 'ladder fiddle yard' as the parallel tracks are likened to the rungs of a ladder. If you can lay track on your layout, you can lay a ladder fiddle yard, and it is not necessary to ballast it either. If you like the electrical and wiring side of the hobby, you can build a diode matrix control panel, whereby pressing just one button sets all the turnouts necessary to reach a particular siding. A ladder fiddle yard is not just for end-to-end layouts – it is perfectly suitable for oval layouts, as you simply repeat the turnouts from the one end at the other.

They are very simple, yet they have one drawback. All those turnouts placed end to end take up a lot of space. A little space can be saved by having shorter turnouts, but not much. The turnouts in a ladder form a series of branches from the main line, and the further out you go, past more and more

This is the extensive ladder fiddle yard on the Warrington Model Railway Club's N gauge exhibition layout, 'Glazebrook'. The length of the tracks means that either one long train or several short trains can be held on each track. Coupled with the number of tracks (serving clockwise and anticlockwise directions), this means that many trains can be sent on to the layout before the first one repeats.

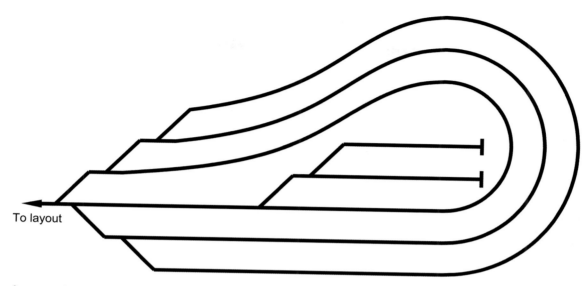

A reverse-loop fiddle yard is a ladder fiddle yard that has been bent back on itself. The advantage is that when used with a terminus layout, the trains can be turned around without any handling, while there is room in the middle for some dead-end tracks for additional storage. It does not need to be as long as a ladder fiddle yard, but it will need to be much deeper.

To layout

turnouts, the shorter the storage sidings become. If you do not use a diode matrix control to 'set the road', you may have a lot of turnouts to set; they are like switches, and if you get just one wrong, you may end up with a collision.

REVERSE-LOOP FIDDLE YARD

An interesting variation of the ladder fiddle yard is the reverse-loop fiddle yard. One of the basic layout shapes is the reverse loop (or dog bone). It is perfectly feasible to add a ladder of sidings around the loop like the layers of an onion, although much more depth needs to be allowed in order to accommodate them, since every extra layer of the onion requires an extra track on both sides of the loop. There is even room within the loop for a ladder of dead-end sidings, or maybe a sector plate.

This design offers plenty of storage, with the ability to reverse complete trains without any handling. Despite the extra depth required for the fiddle yard, it may be ideal for a portable layout that can be erected in a room where the space required on a temporary basis is not an issue. Try telling your model

railway friends that your layout uses a 'reverse-loop onion dog bone fiddle yard with terminal sector-plate storage for hands-off continuous running'.

TRAVERSER

What if you could have the storage capabilities of a ladder of sidings, but without the complication of all those turnouts and the space that they waste? The answer is that you can and the solution is called a traverser. Real railways have used traversers, though only to move little more than a locomotive. A traverser consists of a number of parallel tracks on a sliding table that moves back and forth. A single track into the fiddle yard aligns with one of these tracks at a time. If the track is double, ensure that all the traverser tracks are spaced the same distance apart as the double tracks. Then, any two tracks will always align with the double track.

A traverser is fairly simple to build and can be nothing more complicated than a top sliding on a series of batons underneath. More complicated systems can be created using drawer runners. One rail of each track can be wired to be permanently

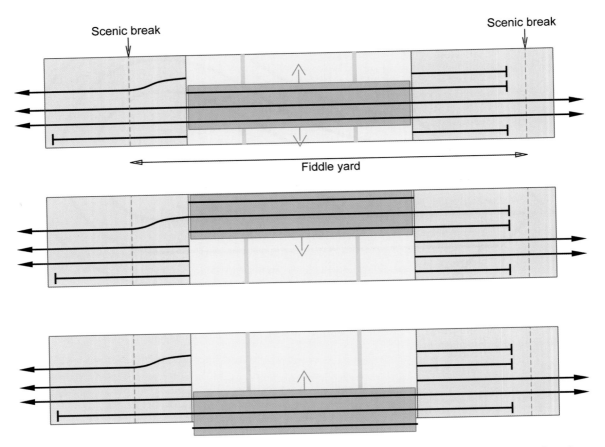

Scenic break

Scenic break

Fiddle yard

A traverser gives the benefits of a ladder fiddle yard without the space taken up by all the turnouts that the latter requires. Trains can also be swapped between tracks without needing any turnouts. The only geometric consideration is that all tracks on a traverser that will align with the through-running lines must be the same distance apart.

live, with section switches to isolate tracks that are not aligned with the main line. Alternatively, use a simple sliding bolt arrangement to secure the traverser in each position, the metal bolt also acting like a switch to energize the track that is aligned.

A traverser is great for both end-to-end and oval layouts, though with the former it is still necessary to reverse the train. While they save a huge amount of space in their length, traversers do consume space in width. Enough space has to be allowed either side of the main line for the traverser to slide into. This is less of a problem where it slides into the aisle, but may be a problem where it slides the other way, especially if the space for the fiddle yard on one side

of the room has been reduced in order to have more room for the scenic side on the other.

SECTOR PLATE

The next solution is a variation on the traverser, which still saves on length by not using turnouts, but does not need quite as much width as a traverser. This is the sector plate, though it is only suitable for end-to-end layouts. A sector plate is pivoted at the end away from the main line to which it connects. A series of tracks are splayed out from the pivot in a series of gentle curves, such that each one will join to the main line when the sector plate is aligned for it. They still require some width, but a little less than a

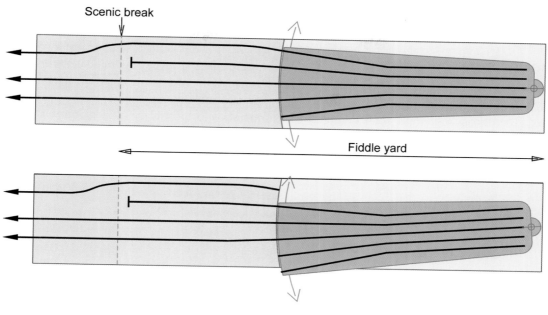

Scenic break

Fiddle yard

ABOVE: *A sector plate is a variation of the traverser, but it can only be used for a terminus-type layout. If more than one track from the layout needs to be connected to the sector plate at the same time, the tracks at the edge of the sector plate must all be the same distance apart.*

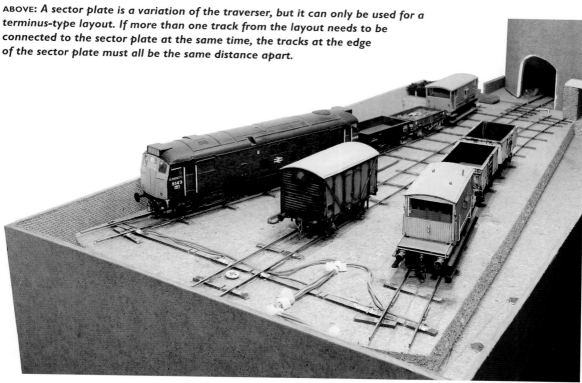

ABOVE: *This OO gauge sector plate was built by Neil Rushby and is simply a solid piece of chipboard pivoted at one end with nothing more complex than a screw. The wires connect to a control panel to allow the individual tracks to be electrically isolated as required. (Photo by Steve Flint, courtesy of Peco Publications and Publicity Ltd)*

traverser, and locomotives still need to be swapped manually from one end to the other.

TURNTABLE

Another variation of the sector plate is to put the pivot in the middle and make a large turntable instead. This allows the whole train to be turned and it can be used on oval as well as end-to-end layouts. It will take up a lot of space since it describes a circle, which means it will need as much depth as length. It is not really a solution for a room-based layout, unless it can be positioned more or less in the middle of the room. You could consider a turntable for a portable layout to be erected temporarily for operation, or possibly as an addition to a bookcase layout, such that it is stored when not in use (though

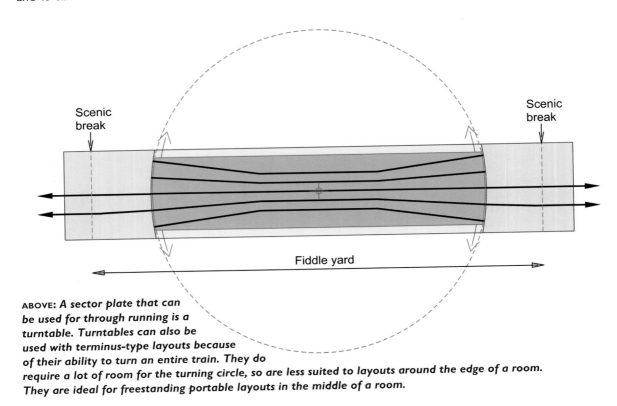

ABOVE: *A sector plate that can be used for through running is a turntable. Turntables can also be used with terminus-type layouts because of their ability to turn an entire train. They do require a lot of room for the turning circle, so are less suited to layouts around the edge of a room. They are ideal for freestanding portable layouts in the middle of a room.*

LEFT: *This view of the train turntable on OO gauge layout 'Buntisland 1883' by the East of Scotland 4mm Group shows that it can be used like a sector plate, but that also it can turn an entire train. Note the guard rails on the side and the lifting gates at the end, which ensure that no stock falls to the ground when the fiddle yard is being turned. (Photo by Steve Flint courtesy of Peco Publications and Publicity Ltd)*

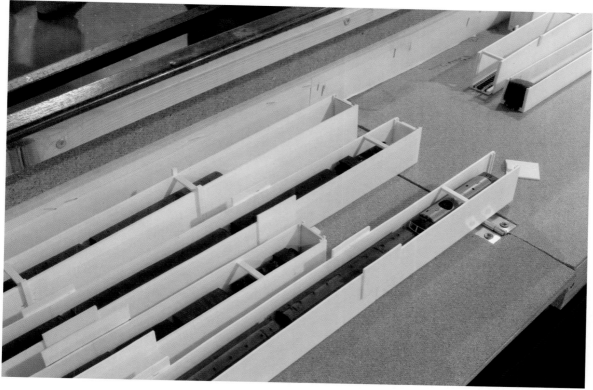

A cassette system such as this one built by Bob Rowlands for his N gauge 'Tetfield-under-Bolt' layout offers maximum flexibility for terminus-type layouts. Trains can be quickly turned and swapped with no need to handle the rolling stock.

the track would likely have to be taken off the end at an angle to allow enough clearance).

CASSETTES

The final fiddle yard solution is the most flexible – this is the cassette system. Just as with video and audio cassettes, the principle is one of being able to remove something safely from the machine in its entirety and replace it with another totally compatible piece. The only commercially available cassette system is Train Safe, a superb system, but at a price. However, as many modellers have proved, it is quite easy to build your own cassette system.

One of the simplest methods is to have pieces of track on the same thickness of material as has been used for the baseboard top. In the fiddle yard, there is another baseboard top, but lower by exactly the thickness of that material. Add simple plywood sides to the cassette to stop the stock falling off as you move it, and there you have it. Another popular method is to use aluminium angle (angled at 90 degrees), which serves as the track, the side protection and the strength of the cassette when it is lifted. The aluminium is simply screwed to a thin wooden base, though care needs to be taken to ensure that the sides stay in gauge all the way along (use a simple wooden template as an aid).

Power to the cassette can be achieved by a number of means. The simplest is to use crocodile clips, which are easy to attach and detach to a terminal on the cassette. Those who use aluminium angle may do this, or may put another piece on the main layout such that when mated with a cassette, a piece of metal channel section is used at the top to lock

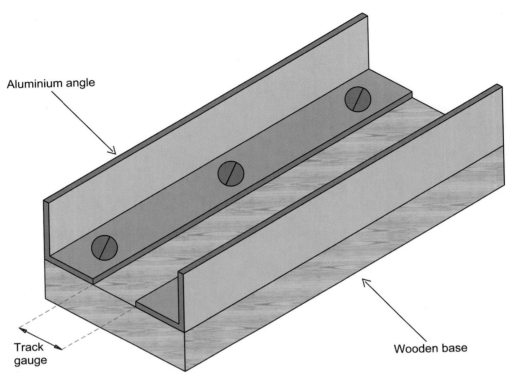

A simple and traditional construction for cassettes is to screw lengths of aluminium angle to pieces of wood. The aluminium angle acts as the track and protects the rolling stock. Power can be supplied to the cassette by simply attaching a wire to each side with crocodile clips.

them in place and bridge the electrical gap. When a cassette is removed, it is automatically disconnected, whatever method has been used to provide power, so there is no fear of the trains driving themselves off. However, it is still good practice to build in some kind of removable buffer for both ends of the cassettes, since given even a slight angle, a train that is not 'braked' by a locomotive will simply roll off.

Cassettes can be any length. You can make them all the same, that is, as long as your longest train, or different lengths for different trains. Why not join cassettes together? Some modellers have short ones for the locomotive, which can then be moved from one end of the train to the other without the locomotive being handled at all. Best of all, the cassette solves the problem of how to turn an entire train without handling the stock, since the whole cassette can be removed and turned in the 'fresh air' above

the layout. There will, though, probably be a practical limit to the length of a cassette that can be handled, certainly if you do want to turn it in its entirety. A ten-coach express train in OO gauge would probably require someone with very long arms.

There is no reason why cassettes cannot be used in the middle of an oval layout, though they do tend to be the preserve of the end-to-end layout. It is for these that they offer a very powerful solution. Just like the single track, they offer a fiddle yard that takes up only a fraction of the space of the layout. They can be easily added to the end of a bookcase layout on a simple stand that collapses out of use when the layout is not being operated. The cassettes are easily removed from the entire layout. They can be stacked, or placed on shelves or racks either above the layout in a room, or underneath if it is a shelf or bookcase layout.

A simple 'socket' arrangement allows cassettes to be 'plugged' into the layout. Note also the removable 'doors' for the ends to make sure that rolling stock does not accidentally fall out. Bob Rowland's 'Tetfield-under-Bolt' layout connects power to the cassettes by simply using rail joiners on the track, which also helps to ensure the alignment of the rails.

COMBINATION SOLUTIONS

Finally, why not mix and match? You could have a few permanent tracks connected by a ladder of turn-outs for your favourite trains, plus one that connects to cassettes to swap other trains. No matter how little space you may think you have, there is always a fiddle yard solution that will handle even the largest of rolling-stock collections. The rest of the world is a big thing, but it does not mean that the fiddle yard that it represents also has to be.

NARROW GAUGE RAILWAYS

Prototype narrow gauge railways come in all shapes and sizes. The broad definition of narrow gauge is any railway where the gauge of the track is less than standard gauge (which is 4ft 8.5in or 1.4m). Think narrow gauge prototype and Welsh slate-carrying railways will first of all come to mind. However, narrow gauge railways could be found all over the United Kingdom, usually short industrial lines (even just within a factory complex), or temporary contractors' railways involved in big construction projects. A narrow gauge line was cheaper and easier to build than standard gauge. It also has one very important advantage for the railway modeller – it will not take up as much space.

Like the prototype, narrow gauge model railways come in all shapes and sizes. Unlike modelling standard gauge (where 'one gauge fits all'), the definition of a narrow gauge scale is a combination of two things – scale and gauge. Broadly speaking, there are two major scale/gauge combinations, which are 7mm scale using OO gauge track and 4mm scale

Narrow gauge railways can use tight curves that do not look out of place on a layout with restricted space, as this view of the Ffestiniog Railway at Porthmadog illustrates.

using N gauge track. The latter is the more popular, undoubtedly due to the greater level of scenic accessories that are available to support OO gauge itself. It is referred to as OO9, where 'OO' refers to 4mm scale and the '9' refers to the track gauge (the 'N' in N gauge means 'nine' millimetres). There are other weird and wonderful combinations of narrow gauge scale/gauge, often described using the American system, which puts a small 'n' between the scale and the prototype gauge. So On3 would be O gauge (or, rather, 7mm scale), running on a model representation of real track that was an actual gauge of 3ft (0.91m).

While discussing scale, as noted above it is a compromise between the level of detail you want to model and the amount you want to fit in. You may want the high level of detail offered by O gauge, yet want the amount of track that only OO gauge can

afford. The answer to this compromise conundrum could be the detail level of 7mm scale combined with OO gauge track by modelling a narrow gauge layout.

Narrow gauge modelling is not as commercially developed as the three major standard gauge scales. There is virtually nothing available ready-to-run; however, there are many suppliers of kits and bits, plus some excellent support from a number of societies. Do not be put off modelling narrow gauge by thinking that it requires experienced kit-building skills. Once again, the use of the smaller track from the commercial scale is an advantage, as the chassis from N gauge models can be used to power OO9 models and those from OO gauge can be used in 7mm scale. Only modest modelling skills are required to make a locomotive body kit. The hard part is constructing a chassis and getting it to run well. By using a ready-to-run chassis, all the hard work is done for you.

Tight corners are often a feature of prototype narrow gauge lines, so a lot can be squeezed into a small space without it looking unrealistic. Tunnels are another feature, especially on Welsh prototypes, so it is easy for the trains to disappear off-stage. This has given rise to the so-called 'rabbit warren' type of layout, where the line constantly disappears into and then reappears from tunnels. These tunnels can be used to break up the layout into individual scenes, so, if you have enough room, you can realistically model an entire narrow gauge railway, for example from slate quarry to port. There seems to be a greater appetite for 'freelancing' in narrow gauge, by inventing your own railway company and mixing and matching the distinctive prototypes from many different railways. It is a branch of railway modelling that possibly offers greater imagination and freedom of expression. These are valuable attributes indeed if you are restricted for space.

TRACK DESIGN ELEMENTS

You may think that track is track and that there is no real science to making a track plan. That is true to some extent, but it is still worth taking a look at the track design elements that can be used in varying numbers to arrive at the track plan of your dreams. Some of them are individual elements, such as sidings, while others are a combination of elements that together make up a new element. For example, a headshunt and a siding combine to make a 'kickback siding'. It is the mixing and matching of these track design elements that give you a working design for your layout.

SIDINGS

You may think that there is nothing to say about something as simple as a set of sidings, yet there are a few things worth noting. On the one hand, you need to provide enough sidings to hold the number of wagons that will be 'delivered' to your layout. Real railways recorded the capacity of sidings and goods yards by the number of wagons that they could hold,

yet it would be rare for them to be full all the time. You can similarly measure how many wagons will fit in the sidings of your layout. However, allow for having a quarter less than that total number on the layout at any one time. This avoids the goods yard looking 'too busy' by being crammed to the gunnels, as well as allowing a little spare capacity in case you bring on a larger wagon such as a bogie well truck. On the other hand, do not be tempted to cram in too many sidings in order to hold as many wagons as possible. Once again, things will start to look unrealistically cramped.

Most sidings in a goods yard will face the same direction. Real railways prefer this as it makes shunting more efficient. If you want to make operation a little more challenging, face some of the sidings in the opposite direction. Having to service two sets of sidings requires at least one run-round manoeuvre. Alternatively, have the goods yard facing one way and a private siding facing the other to serve, for example, a factory. However, running sidings each way from a central point will require either a longer layout or shorter sidings.

Sidings that are used to store rolling stock or for marshalling can be quite close together. They only require enough room for a shunter to walk between them to take the wagon brakes on or off. Goods yard sidings would be much further apart to allow access for carts and lorries to deliver and receive goods. This spreading out requires a greater depth to the baseboard. If sufficient depth is not available, you may have to lose one of the sidings altogether.

HEADSHUNT

A headshunt is a length of track that allows a shunting locomotive to draw wagons clear of one siding in order to propel them into another. Real headshunts are used where shunting is required next to a busy main line, as it saves the need for the shunting locomotive continually to have to use the main line as a headshunt. A headshunt needs to be as long as the locomotive plus the maximum number of wagons that may be needed to draw out of the sidings in one go. This can lead to it being quite a length in real life. Using the principle of selective compression,

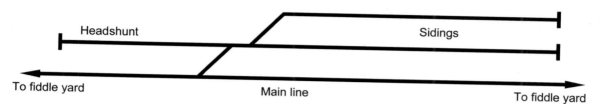

A headshunt allows the shunting of sidings to proceed without the need to use the main line, which would require shunting to stop every time a train passed by.

In an industrial or urban setting, the length of a buffer stop on a siding or headshunt can be saved by using a track that actually goes nowhere. The door on this building implies that the track enters inside; however, the model door does not open. This saves the length of the buffer stop seen on the siding on the left. There is a substantial block of wood behind the door in case an operator tries to drive the locomotive through it.

OPPOSITE: *A typical goods yard with a fan of sidings. It is clear how having to allow for the turnouts means that each siding gets progressively shorter. The last one at the top right is a kickback into a motive power depot.*

the headshunt can be made shorter than real life. It might frustrate a real railway company, but for those of us seeking challenging operation, it is actually a bonus.

A headshunt can be a siding itself. That does mean that any wagons in the siding for unloading must be moved out of the way before the track can be used as a headshunt. Then they have to be returned afterwards as well. For prototype railways, this sort of operation is a real headache, but for railway modellers it just adds to the fun.

On smaller end-to-end layouts, there may not be enough room for a workable-length headshunt without making the sidings rather short. In this case, the headshunt can be run into the fiddle yard parallel to the fiddle yard tracks. This is even easier if the fiddle yard is a traverser, as one of the traverser tracks can be lined up as the headshunt. This approach has the advantage that you can have a decent length of headshunt while still having longer sidings on the layout. The disadvantage is that the locomotive will keep disappearing off the layout when shunting is in progress, although at least some wagons will always be visible.

LOOP THE LOOP

Unless you construct a very simple fan of sidings, such as 'Inglenook Sidings', it is likely that after your train arrives from the fiddle yard, the loco will need to 'run round' to return from whence it came. So a run-round loop is the first essential requirement for a layout. Even a through station can have a need for a loop, either to let trains pass, or to shunt a goods yard.

How long should the loop be? Knowing the size of the longest wagon or coach, the length needs to be approximate multiples of that depending on how many wagons or coaches you want to run round. However, this does not limit train length to what can be fitted in the loop and this is where the enjoyment of shunting comes in. If your train is longer, part of it can be left on a different siding while you run round the rest. It is a personal choice how complicated you want to make it. Adding an extra turnout at each end of the loop instantly gives a couple of sidings. These can serve a goods shed, coal merchant, factory and so on.

These loops are very traditional and economical for through-running and narrow baseboards. To make things a little more challenging in a terminus situation, try putting a line that runs into one side of the run-round loop. Most trains will run through the side of the loop to the headshunt and then have to reverse the train into the loop in order to run round.

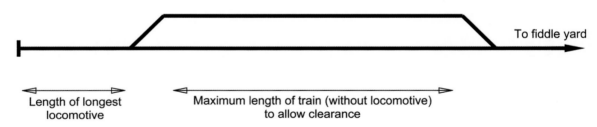

A simple run-round loop allows a locomotive to swap ends for a return journey from a terminus. The key measurements are to allow enough room for your longest locomotive, plus the longest train (without locomotive) that you will use.

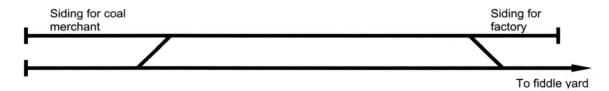

By using a single platform as befits a country station terminus or an island platform between the tracks, sidings can be added at the ends of the run-round loop to serve freight customers.

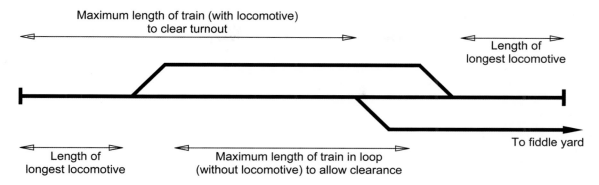

A more operationally challenging run-round loop is one where the arriving train has to reverse into the loop before the run-round can take place. This requires an additional measurement, that of the maximum length of train plus locomotive in order to clear the turnout from the fiddle yard.

THE KICKBACK SIDING

A kickback siding is a siding that 'kicks back' in the opposite direction from another siding. A locomotive has to run into the first siding (in effect, a headshunt) with a wagon in tow and then reverse into the kickback siding, propelling the wagon. This is easy enough, but let's start to make life difficult for the driver. First, make the main siding shorter than the kickback siding. If the kickback siding will take four wagons but the main siding will only take two (or one wagon and one loco), then you can only get one wagon into the kickback at a time. If the wagons have to be delivered to the kickback siding in a particular order, this requires more shunting.

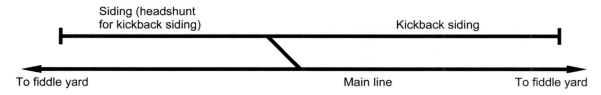

A kickback siding 'kicks back' off another siding. The first siding has to be cleared in order to act as a headshunt for the kickback siding. They are therefore operationally challenging, but that's part of the fun.

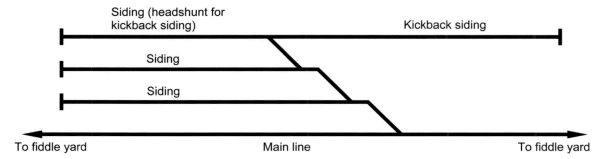

A fan of sidings will become progressively shorter due to the space required for turnouts. A kickback siding helps to fill some of the void this creates by sending track back the other way.

Kickback sidings are popular on American switching (shunting) layouts. In this example, the blue wagon at the top left has been moved all the way to the end of the siding (headshunt) to allow room for the locomotive and green wagon to access the kickback siding.

You can kickback a siding from any other siding. For example, you can have a fan of three sidings and the last one can kickback. This is useful so as to put some track into the void created by the turnouts placed one after another to achieve the fan of sidings.

PENDULUM SIDINGS

This is a set of sidings (also known as switchback sidings) whereby one siding is a headshunt into another siding, which itself is a headshunt into another siding and so on. The effect is to swing from one end of the yard to the other while gradually moving towards the front. This is a very inefficient way of building a yard in real life, yet it is huge fun for the railway modeller looking for challenging operation.

CROSSOVERS

A different, and slightly easier to operate, version of the kickback siding is to put two sidings 'toe to toe'. However, on compact layouts, this can waste a lot of space as the two sidings can be quite short. The left-hand siding can be made longer by moving

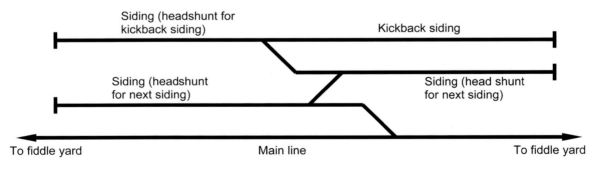

Pendulum (or switchback) sidings are a set of successive kickback sidings that require the locomotive to keep changing direction in order to reach the furthest siding. Real railways would avoid them as they are hugely inflexible and inefficient; however, they allow layout designers to distribute track evenly over the layout as well as providing challenging operation.

To reach the provender hut (numbered six) at the bottom right from the large shed at the top left (numbered one) requires five moves and four changes of direction. However, it does mean a lot of movement in such a short space. To travel an equivalent distance in a straight line would require a layout that was at least three times longer than this one.

the left-hand turnout further right and the same for the right-hand siding. However, the sidings will now cross over each other. So, by using one of the readily available crossovers, the sidings are now longer, but you have to remember not to leave wagons fouling the crossover.

A number of model track manufacturers make crossovers. These crossovers are measured in degrees, in other words, the angle between the crossing tracks. Alternatively, for greater operational flexibility, you could use either a single or double slip, though be aware that these are complex pieces of turnout engineering in model form as much as in real life. They usually come with electrified frogs, which means that the wiring required can be quite challenging.

BAY PLATFORM

A bay platform is usually a shorter platform at the side of a main platform. Bay platforms were often a feature of rural branch-line terminus stations, as they allowed another platform face without the need to build an additional platform on the opposite side. They were not just a feature of branch-line termini; they could be found in town and city stations. Some larger through stations have a bay platform for services that terminate there; indeed, such facilities could have two faces and even a run-round loop.

WAGON TURNTABLES

When we think of a railway turntable, what usually springs to mind is a large metal construction over a

On my very compact N gauge industrial shunting layout called 'Mill Lane Sidings', the sidings at the top would have been very short if the turnouts had been arranged 'toe to toe'. By reversing the turnouts and adding a crossover, the sidings are much longer. From the turnout, their length is almost two-thirds of the length of the layout.

Bay platforms can be quite short, in this case just long enough to hold a Great Western auto-train of one coach and one locomotive. Trains such as this and diesel or electric multiple units do not require a run-round loop for the return journey. This offers a lot of space-saving potential.

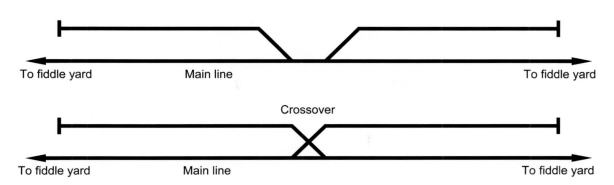

To fiddle yard   Main line   To fiddle yard

Crossover

To fiddle yard   Main line   To fiddle yard

Another favourite of American modelling is to use a crossover. Swapping the position of the turnouts for the sidings in the top diagram means that the sidings cross over each other in the bottom diagram; however, it makes the sidings slightly longer.

pit that is capable of turning a heavy steam locomotive. Yet the most common form of turntable was the smaller wooden variety that was just big enough to take a 9ft (2.7m) wheelbase goods van or coal wagon. They were used extensively in goods yards and factories, not to turn wagons round, but to turn them through 90 degrees, effectively making a sharp turn to the left or right. Even real railways realized the importance of being able to manipulate wagons in the smallest of spaces. Obviously, a locomotive could not move the wagon in this way, although it could pull the wagons with a rope via a capstan. More usual was to use one of the thousands of shunting horses that once moved as much around yards as locomotives did.

For the railway modeller, the wagon turntable would be a brilliant space-saving device; however, how do you replicate the operation in miniature? The turntable itself is fairly easy, but getting an OO gauge horse to haul the wagon into a shed might be beyond even the best modellers. Some have attempted to mechanize the operation (though not with a horse), utilizing either a magnet under the baseboard to move the wagon, or a hook that comes out of the shed to pull the wagon inside. The wagon turntable really is a useful device, so in order not to miss out on it, perhaps the simplest thing is to resort to the oldest method of all – move the wagon by your own fair hand.

CHAPTER THREE

BASIC LAYOUT SHAPES

A model railway layout can be any shape or size. There are no prescriptive rules for what a design should or should not be. However, there are common themes that consistently crop up, so it is worth taking a look at the most common shapes of layouts. They are referred to all the time in this book and you will see them time and again in model railway magazines and at exhibitions.

OVAL LAYOUTS

If you had a train set when you were younger, it's a sure bet that it came with an oval of track. This is basically a circle of track with some straight pieces to split it into two and elongate it into an oval. It is wonderfully simple to supply with the train set and for eager little fingers to put together. Within a few minutes, you have something that lets the trains run round ad infinitum.

An OO gauge oval can just about fit on to a baseboard that will go on a tabletop, though it is a little limiting regarding what can be done in terms of stations, sidings and so on. The oval starts to develop its full potential when it gets physically bigger — big enough, in fact, that you can stand in the middle of it while the trains run around you. If you have a room-sized space in which to build a layout, the oval is a natural fit. Most room-sized spaces are broadly rectangular, which maps superbly to the oval. A fiddle yard is usually placed on one side with a scenic focus on the other. This layout shape is great for maximizing a modest room-sized space — just sit back and watch the trains go by.

TERMINUS LAYOUTS

Railways can be thought of as either travelling through somewhere, or travelling to somewhere. The oval layout is perfect for a scene that you want the railway (and the trains) to pass through from one

place to another. On the other hand, if you want a feeling of arrival, of trains travelling to a final destination, then you can do no better than to model a terminus. If you do not have the space for an oval layout, the terminus shape is slimmer and more adaptable to less space. It is suitable for both permanent and portable situations, whether you have just one wall available, or a tabletop or a piece of furniture.

The word 'terminus' conjures up an image of vast city stations like Waterloo, Euston and King's Cross. But a terminus is basically any 'dead-end', simply the end of the line. By definition, a branch line 'branches off' and many of them did not join up with the rest of the railway network somewhere else. Think of the Great Western Railway branch-line termini, ever popular with modellers. They are charming, of course, in their bucolic setting in the countryside, but much of their appeal lies in the simplicity of the track plan that still manages to offer passenger and goods services, sometimes even modest locomotive facilities.

A terminus does not have to be a station at all. It is simply the end of a line. Even a goods yard or a motive power depot can be regarded as a terminus. While such facilities are usually situated alongside a line, very often it is just one siding off the main line that leads into a yard. There are examples of yards and motive power depots that are seemingly in the middle of nowhere, removed from the main railway, especially in cramped urban situations where real estate was hard to come by. Factories, coal mines and quarries are further examples of 'long sidings' often several miles from the main line, but basically, they are a terminus. With a little research, you can find prototype inspiration that is a little different — truly 'off the beaten track'.

Some modellers may not favour a terminus shape because the trains cannot be left to their own devices as they would be when running around an oval for

End of the line – a terminus layout such as 'Parkhouse', built by Stephen Farmer in N gauge, can be compact, yet both realistic and atmospheric. Note the clever use of an island platform to give two platform faces, served by DMUs that do not require a run-round loop.

hours on end. Yet what you lose in the simplicity of an oval, you gain in the challenge of operation. Although the distance from the fiddle yard to the terminus may not be that long a journey, once you get there, you face all the fun of fitting trains into platforms and goods yards, run-round operations and preparing the trains to send them back to the fiddle yard again.

Perhaps more than any other layout shape, the terminus can occupy as little or as much space as you want or have available. It is perfectly feasible to build a terminus layout in a rectangular-shaped room, with the station on one side and a fiddle yard

on the other, each sited down the longer wall and joined by a half circle at one end to form a giant U-shape. At the other end of the scale, you need little more than a plank with a station at one end and fiddle yard at the other. Such a small layout is easily integrated into a piece of furniture, stored (or indeed operated) on a shelf, or packed away into a cupboard when not in use. It is one of the best friends of the space-starved modeller.

The terminus shape assumes a destination at one end and a fiddle yard at the other. The use of the fiddle yard with the terminus (and any layout shape for that matter) allows trains to be easily stored and changed so that an interesting variety of trains can be brought on and off the layout. The fiddle yard represents the rest of the railway network. However, consider building a terminus-to-terminus layout. This tends to be less common with standard gauge modellers, who prefer the flexibility offered by the option of the 'rest of the railway network' in a fiddle yard. It is, though, very suitable to narrow gauge and industrial modellers. The prototype inspirations for such models were very often small concerns, sometimes only travelling a few miles. Consider a narrow gauge railway carrying slate from a quarry in the hills down to a harbour on the coast. Such railways, although often quite a few miles long, were basically closed systems from one terminus to another. There is a lot of prototype inspiration to be found in the history of many real railways, both large and small.

The terminus shape offers lots of operational enjoyment, with perhaps a few more design challenges, such as fiddle yards and making sure that you design a track plan with enough 'play value' to keep you interested once the layout is built. Yet more so than any layout shape, it is versatile and can be fitted into any available permanent or portable space. Of the classic and still popular designs that are suitable for restricted-space situations, it is no coincidence that they are all termini.

DOG BONES AND REVERSE LOOPS

If you do not have room for a layout that loops around a room (you may only have one wall of a room available), you could be forgiven for thinking that your only option is to have a terminus layout. But if you still want to sit back and watch the trains go by, there is another alternative, which is to put a loop at each end of the layout. This type of layout is sometimes called a 'dog bone', for obvious reasons, and the loops at each end are, equally logically, called 'reverse loops'.

The simplest way to reverse the loop is in conjunction with a double-track main line on the through tracks. One of these tracks enters the loop, and because the loop comes back, it becomes the

track on the other side, but now running the other way. The easiest way to think of this is to imagine taking the traditional oval shape and pinching it in the middle until the straight tracks either side are almost touching. So the simple dog bone layout is actually an oval layout in disguise.

If you want the through track to be just a single track, the loops are easy to construct, as you simply use a turnout to join the loop back to the through track. However, the electrical wiring is a little more involved, as the polarity of the track in the loop needs to be reversed. This is not as difficult as it sounds. A two-rail system has a positive rail and a negative rail. By wrapping the loop track back to the through track, the outer rail is positive going into the loop, but it has to be negative when it comes out of the loop, as it is now joined to the negative rail on the other side of the through track. There are several ways to do this. You can just stop the train and throw a switch to change the polarity as you switch the turnout (remember to swap the direction on the controller as well). Slightly more complex is to combine the polarity switch with the turnout switch. There are electronic modules available that will do all of this for you. The best is to use DCC, since a DCC locomotive literally goes forwards in the direction that it physically faces. Therefore, while you still have to change polarity in the loop, you do not have to change the direction on your controller. Once again, you can buy DCC modules that will do all the hard work for you, while negating the need to stop the train in the loop.

You will need to carefully measure the available depth for each loop. This is because at least twice the minimum radius of your chosen scale will be required, as virtually a full circle of track will be needed in order to achieve the reverse loop. If you model in OO gauge, for example, and your minimum radius is 18in (46cm), you will need 36in (which is 3ft, or about 1m). The through track between the reverse loops can meet the loop in the centre of a circle, or be flat on one side with a half circle and reverse curve (basically, an S-shape) on the other. The latter means that the through tracks can be close to the wall and take up little depth. However, if

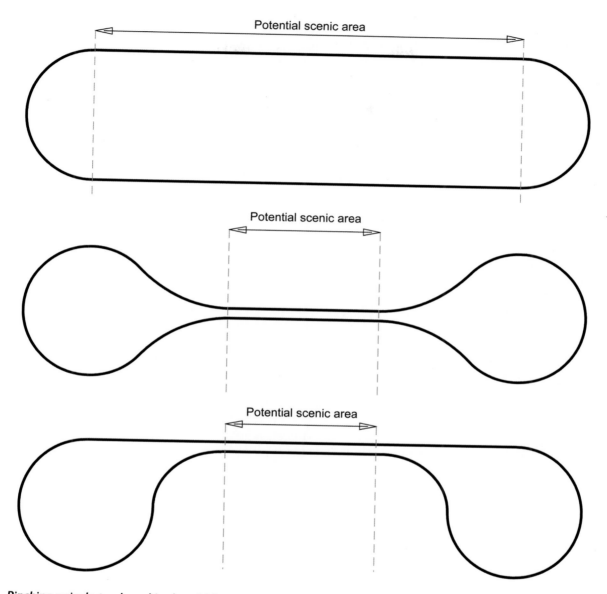

Potential scenic area

Potential scenic area

Potential scenic area

Pinching a single-track oval in the middle converts it into a dog bone shape with a double track in the middle. Trains will then be able to pass one way through the scenic area, then back in the opposite direction. The trade-off is a significant reduction in the amount of scenic area available in order to maintain the double-track illusion. Squeezing the oval from just one side keeps the other side flat, leaving much more room in front of the track.

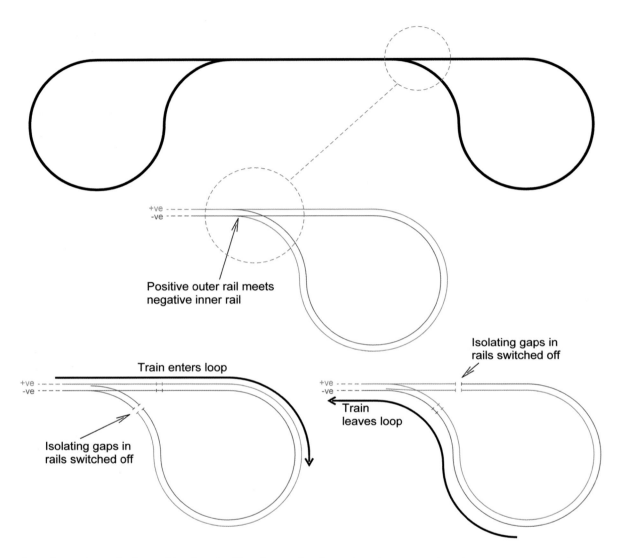

+ve - - - -
-ve - - - -

Positive outer rail meets
negative inner rail

Isolating gaps in
rails switched off

Train enters loop

+ve - - - -
-ve - - - -

Isolating gaps in
rails switched off

+ve - - - -
-ve - - - -

Train
leaves loop

A single track can be looped back to itself to form a dog bone, but this means that the positive outer rail conflicts with the negative inner rail. The solution is to fit insulating gaps at the start and end of the loop, which are switched on and off in conjunction with the direction of the turnout. The train has to be stopped in the loop to change the direction on the controller unless a proprietary polarity-changing module is used.

you have to allow for the depth of the reverse loops at each end, that depth in the middle can be used for scenic possibilities, or perhaps a number of sidings.

L-SHAPES AND U-SHAPES

If an oval shape favours all four walls of a room, while a terminus shape needs only a minimum of

just one, then L-shape and U-shape layouts fall somewhere in-between. You may have a permanent location for a layout in a room; however, you may still need to share the room with another function, so that you do not have access to all the walls, or all of the space on the walls. If this is the case, you can take a terminus shape and either bend it in half to create an L-shape, or bend it into three and create a U-shape, either of which will hug the available wall space.

Everything that was said earlier about the terminus shape applies equally well here, though the implication is that a little more space is available. However, bear in mind that each of the 'bends' to make an L-shape or a U-shape is actually a quarter-circle to take the track through 90 degrees. It is not impossible to put such a bend in the middle of a platform, but it could be problematic, especially if the corners use the tightest radius possible. Therefore, the bends are more likely to be used to separate sections of the layout. On an L-shape, it is likely that your terminus will occupy the longer side of the 'L', while the fiddle yard is on the other (shorter) side and they are joined by the bend. With a U-shape, the same applies, but the bottom of the 'U' could host another feature such as a goods yard, factory or motive power depot.

Finally, remember that a dog bone shape can also be adapted to be either an L-shape or a U-shape. However, it would probably suit the former more than the latter. With a U-shape, by the time you have allowed enough space at each end of the 'U' for the reverse loops, you might as well just join them together into a loop. The L-shape possibly offers the greatest potential for using a dog bone against

more than one wall. In fact, it offers the beginnings of breaking away from the traditional shapes outlined so far.

PENINSULA-BASED LAYOUTS

If you read any railway modelling books or magazines and study the track plans they contain, you are sure to see plenty of examples of the layout shapes that have been described so far. However, there are no rules that say that a layout must be an oval shape or a terminus. Of course, the space available can define a shape and dictate the eventual layout shape. If all you have is a corner of a room, you are pretty much stuck with an L-shape. But when a moderate room-sized space is available, you don't have to constrain yourself to traditional thinking.

There are some very good ideas in North American model railway thinking that seek to maximize the space available. It is worth studying one aspect of the American model railway philosophy now as we look at layout shape. American modellers like a lot of track, not in the sense of filling every square foot with as much as possible, but in terms of achieving as much main-line run as possible. The operation-oriented American modeller wants as long a line as possible in order to have as

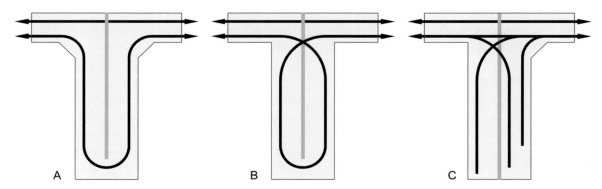

Three examples of peninsula baseboards that extend into the aisle to form a T-shape. With A, the main-line run is extended by simply running down the peninsula and back again. A scenic divider goes down the middle as far as the curve to separate the peninsula into two landscapes. Example B is similar, except that the main line passes through the scenic divider and crosses over itself (either using a bridge or a crossover). Through-running remains on the main baseboard in Example C and the peninsula is now used as a terminus. The scenic divider is optional and offers the chance to have two separate termini.

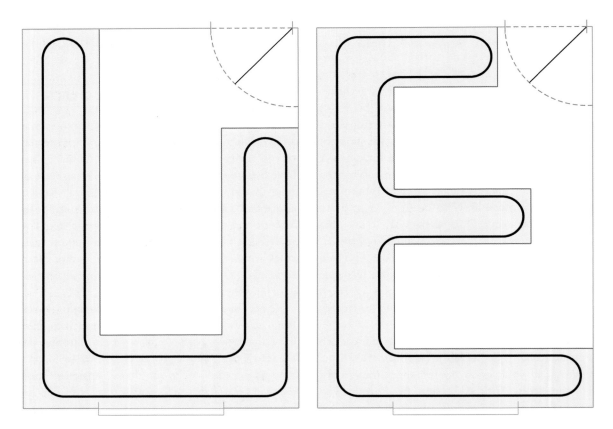

A typical room shape with a corner door at one end and a window at the other. The baseboard arrangement on the left is a typical U-shape. On the right, the U-shape has been turned through 90 degrees and overlaid with a T-shaped peninsula to form an E-shape. The length of track is virtually identical in both plans, but the E-shape offers a potentially more interesting layout.

many stations and industries along it. Admittedly, a lot of Americans have very large basements in which to achieve this; however, it is worth studying how they pack in the main line. There are lots of smaller room-sized plans published, as even Americans recognize that not everyone has masses of space. Many of these plans are simply mindboggling in their complexity to modellers in the UK. The one thing not seen very often is a simple oval.

One of the concepts used often is a peninsula. This juts out within the oval and can be either a narrow board that forms a terminus, or slightly wider to allow a loop (the design considerations of reverse loops apply here, although the train is not being sent back on itself). Alternatively, imagine laying a T-shape

over a U-shape (the result being an E-shape). Rather than fitting the U-shape so that the tails are against the longer walls, turn it though 90 degrees so that the bottom of the 'U' is on one of the longer walls. The T-shape then fits in the middle. It might not seem to offer that much extra track, but it does offer the illusion of greater distance between stations. If combined with dog bone reverse loops, with the return track largely hidden at the rear, there is the potential for continuous running over a considerable distance.

Do remember to allow enough room so that you can get around the layout, especially if you are going to have friends round to operate it. The aisles around a peninsula can become pinch points – the last thing you want is for it to be necessary for one person to leave the room so that another can get out from an aisle.

The peninsula style layout encourages the operator to follow the train and walk round with it (DCC control is ideal, as the controller can be plugged in at different places without having to stop the train). One of the key concepts of the peninsula shape is a scenic divider down the middle of the peninsula. It is more than a back scene, but it may stop short before the end of the peninsula where the line loops round. It is literally a scenic divide, separating one side of the peninsula from the other.

One thing is for sure, and that is that American modellers are the masters of imaginative track geometry. Even if you do not want the operationally intensive type of layout that they are striving for, do study how they design track plans and frame a long, continuous scene with dividers. It is always worth looking at how someone else is approaching the same problems that you face and a peek 'over the pond' is to be thoroughly recommended.

DOUBLE-SIDED LAYOUTS

Your potential space may have quite a bit of depth, but not a lot of length. This is likely to be the situation with, for example, a tabletop layout. In such situations, think about building a double-sided layout. This has a back scene down the middle of the baseboard that splits the layout into two halves. The basic version of this is an oval layout with a station at the front and a fiddle yard at the rear. The back scene does the important job of separating the modelled world of the scenic half from the artificial world of the fiddle yard. If you are content to run the same train most of the time, then you do not need a fiddle yard at all and the back scene serves to separate two totally distinct scenes – perhaps rural on one side and urban on the other.

You are not restricted to oval designs if you want to have a double-sided layout – for example, one end of the oval can be chopped off to create a U-shape. Once again, the central back scene separates the two halves. You can build a terminus to fiddle yard

type of layout, or build two termini – an end-to-end layout can actually be built in a rectangle. Curves take up quite a lot of 'real estate', but the tighter the radius, the more difficulties this may create. It is good to know, then, that there are even more radical ways of building a double-sided layout. These designs do away with curves altogether.

The basic concept of a double-sided layout that uses no curves is to join the two halves of the baseboard by taking a track through the middle of the back scene. Such an approach may not leave enough room for a station on either side unless using a smaller scale like N gauge, plus the tabletop is of a reasonable size. Therefore, it may be more suitable to shunting layouts where there are short headshunts and lots of sidings. For example, you could model part of a colliery on one side with a gasworks on the other. There is a natural synergy there between a supplier (the colliery) and the customer (the gasworks), with a flow of loaded wagons one way and empties in the opposite direction.

Without a fiddle yard, though, there may be some limitations. Gasworks actually produce by-products such as tar, which can be dispatched by rail, but a colliery would not be a customer. Similarly, the colliery requires wagon-loads of pit props, which the gasworks cannot supply. But there are still plenty of possible and workable examples for this design. How about a narrow gauge railway feeding slate from the quarries on one side to the docks on the other? Even in standard gauge, you could have a dockyard on one side and a goods yard on the other – ports often had short branch lines from the main goods yard by the station to the dockyard. If you like short goods trains and lots of shunting, there must be endless possibilities for the self-contained end-to-end layout to be explored.

If, however, you want to be able to inject more variety into operations by using a fiddle yard to get trains on and off the layout, consider putting the fiddle yard in the middle of the layout, literally in the back scene (actually two back scenes with a fiddle yard between them). The gap for the fiddle yard on the baseboard would be too narrow to be practical, so here are two solutions. First, run the track

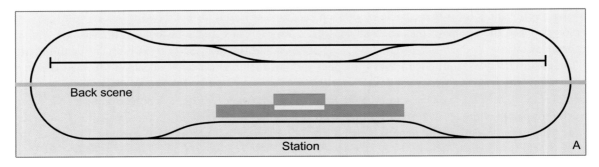

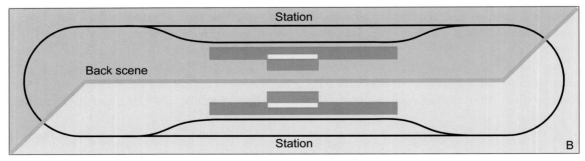

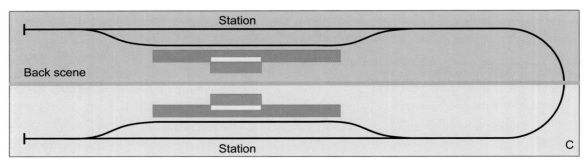

The traditional simple double-sided layout uses an oval or U-shape. Plan A is a simple oval with a station on one side and a fiddle yard on the other; the back scene down the middle separates the two. Plan B is similar, but the fiddle yard has been replaced with another station. Also, the back scene has been changed to an elongated S-shape to break up some of the straight lines. Plan C is a U-shape terminus to terminus layout. As with Plan A, one of the stations could be a fiddle yard and, like Plan B, there are no rules about the position or shape of the back scene.

to the edge of the baseboard and connect it to any kind of fiddle yard. This temporary baseboard can be connected to the layout for operating sessions as long as there is space for it. If it overhangs the tabletop, one end can be supported with a simple folding leg arrangement. Secondly, by using a cassette system, the cassette can be inserted into the gap and connected to the track that feeds both sides.

The cassettes act as a headshunt, a means to transfer trains between the two scenic halves, plus a way to swap rolling stock from the layout as a whole.

COMBINATION SHAPES

Having looked at the common layout shapes such as ovals and termini, and then studied how they can be

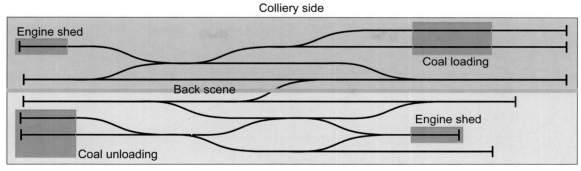

This double-sided layout is two shunting-type layouts either side of a central back scene. They are joined by a crossover that passes through the middle of the back scene. Although the hole in the back scene for the track is now very much in the centre of both layouts, it is easily disguised by using buildings or view blockers.

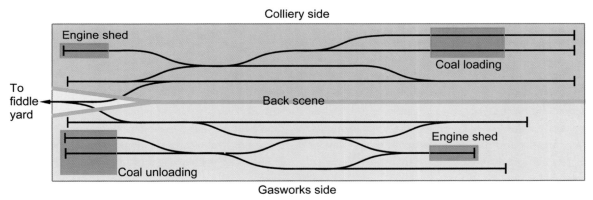

A development of the colliery to gasworks double-sided layout is to make it slightly deeper so as to add a common connection at one end to a fiddle yard solution such as a sector plate. This allows more operational flexibility in getting rolling stock on and off the layout, although the additional length of a fiddle yard may mean that the layout no longer fits on a table.

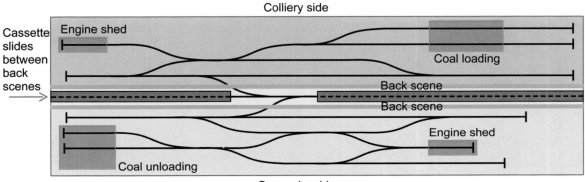

The final design for the colliery to gasworks double-sided layout is to use two parallel back scenes down the middle of the layout into which can be inserted cassettes. These act as a headshunt between the two halves of the layout, plus a simple means of changing rolling stock. There is none of the additional overhang of a separate fiddle yard, which makes this an excellent tabletop solution.

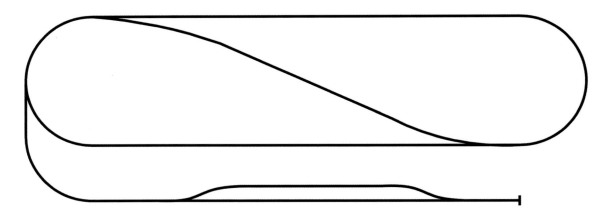

This is a deceptively simple layout plan that is a combination of three basic layout shapes. There is a straightforward oval at the top and a basic terminus at the bottom, but the third shape may be harder to spot. The track that runs diagonally from one corner of the loop to the other forms a reverse loop, which permits 'out and back' running from the terminus. A train can leave the terminus, run clockwise around the loop, take the diagonal to reverse direction, run anticlockwise around the loop and then arrive back at the terminus.

altered to make other shapes, the final point to make is that the basic layout shapes can be combined to make any shape you like. Just like the track elements, you can mix and match and adapt the basic layout shapes until you have the design that gives you what you want in the space available.

The most common combination will probably be to join an oval and a terminus. A layout can be a series of layers, basically how one part of a layout can be placed over another. The simplest of these combinations is to put a terminus over part of an oval and link them together at a junction. Alternatively, you could keep everything on the level and include a

terminus inside, or (less commonly) outside an oval. Perhaps there is room for more than one terminus. Don't forget that a terminus does not have to be a station; it could be an industry or a goods yard. These small termini are a lot easier to fit in all over the layout.

The basic layout shapes are essentially just layout building blocks. They will give you an idea of what you can do and put other people's layout designs into context. But do not feel that you should be restricted to familiar shapes. A healthy dose of imagination will allow you to shape the layout you want in the space you have, not the other way around.

CHAPTER FOUR

THE ART OF COMPROMISE

All layouts are a compromise, some more than others. When taking into consideration that you must balance your skill (in multiple disciplines from woodwork to electrical wiring), spare time, money and of course, available space, you know that you're going to have to make some compromises somewhere. You may want beautiful hand-built track, but without the time to build it, you compromise and purchase ready-made flexible track. Perhaps you want a large fleet of DCC sound-equipped locomotives, but you don't have the money. You would like a layout the size of a football field, yet only have the space on top of the dining table. There is nothing wrong with a few pipedreams, but reality has to bite at some point.

Do not focus first of all on fitting the layout you would like into the space you have available, as you will spend all your time trimming it back to fit. This will become disheartening after a while as you prune more and more of your grand dream. Instead, focus on what you would like a layout to achieve. This is referred to as 'reverse engineering', the idea that you work backwards from the desired result. Otherwise, you will end up saying, 'if I was going there, I wouldn't start from here'.

TAKE A WALK DOWN THE AISLE

Will your model railway be a solitary affair, or will you want to invite your family and friends to join you? You may have a design in mind that fits into the available space, but have you considered allowing space for extra bodies other than your own? What is the maximum number of guests you may have and will they fit into the space? In a layout based in a spare room, this may mean relinquishing one wall of layout in order to allow enough breathing space (literally) for people. The minimum comfortable aisle width is 2.5ft (0.76m).

If you are a very social modeller and have many acquaintances with whom to share your fun, consider abandoning the spare room and taking one of the 'furniture layout' options. This will allow you to have a modest layout that assembles in a bigger room – a much more convivial atmosphere and some decent armchairs as well. You may lose a lot of the layout you wanted, but the compensation for this compromise is being able to build a layout that is more sociable in its operation.

Once the layout is constructed, you will likely be sitting down to operate it and you will have the opportunity to swing your legs under the baseboard, as if you were sitting at a table. If you are unsure what will be comfortable for you, try mocking up the available space using the kitchen table and a few chairs before cutting any timber for actual baseboards. It is also worth considering an office chair (so-called 'five-star' chairs as they have five casters), as these will allow you to swivel from one side to the other and easily swing your legs under the baseboards, plus they are height-adjustable. Such chairs can be obtained very cheaply, but do not skimp too much – remember that you want to be spending many a comfortable hour enjoying your model railway.

WISH LISTS

You might wish that you could model an entire main line with every station and goods yard, but unless you have a winning lottery ticket, it is a wish that must sadly remain a dream. However, there is no reason not to still have a wish list for the layout that you want to build. By taking a few minutes to work up a wish list, disappointments and frustrations can be avoided further down the line.

First of all, what sort of layout do you want? If you want to sit and relax watching trains go by, you probably want an oval layout with a fiddle yard supplying

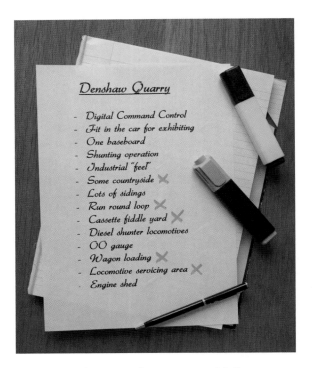

Denshaw Quarry

- Digital Command Control
- Fit in the car for exhibiting
- One baseboard
- Shunting operation
- Industrial "feel"
- Some countryside ✗
- Lots of sidings
- Run round loop ✗
- Cassette fiddle yard ✗
- Diesel shunter locomotives
- OO gauge
- Wagon loading ✗
- Locomotive servicing area ✗
- Engine shed

The only tools you need to create a wish list are pens and paper. This is the original wish list that was created for my 'Denshaw Quarry' layout, complete with ticks and crosses to show what was personally most important. Some things are interrelated – fitting Digital Command Control into small shunting locos requires OO gauge as a minimum, but a larger scale would not fit on one baseboard in the back of the car (to take to exhibitions).

a variety of trains. If you enjoy shunting puzzles and running freight trains, you will likely want a goods yard. If you have a large collection of locomotives that you wish to display, how about a motive power depot?

Next, what sort of modelling do you want to do? Are you happy to use ready-made scenery and rolling stock? Or do you enjoy making kits and adding the high levels of detail that are possible in the larger scales? Consider that scratch-building every last detail with the fewest commercial components is a very satisfying branch of the hobby, but possibly not one for large layouts due to the time involved. At the other extreme, the more that's purchased

ready-made, the more can be achieved in a shorter time.

Time is an important factor, especially these days. Even if you are retired and looking for a hobby, most retired people claim to be busier than when they were working. If you want instant gratification, then a modest layout with mostly ready-made items is the route to take. On the other hand, if you want a long-term project to keep you more occupied with the making than the operation, consider a larger project. Large does not necessarily mean more space, as kit-building and scratch-building are something that require large amounts of time and commitment.

Writing a wish list may seem like overkill for what is after all going to be a hobby, especially if you are new to railway modelling. Yet it is all the more helpful if you are a newcomer, since it will stop you going off in the wrong direction. All model railways have to compromise in one area or another, so the wish list is the vital starting point towards limiting the degree of compromise.

IDENTIFYING WHAT IS MOST IMPORTANT TO YOU

Once you have a wish list, compare how some of its elements map to the space that you have available. Obviously, if you want a four-track main line with highly detailed O gauge locomotives yet only have a bookcase available, you may think that you have fallen at the first hurdle. However, by clearly identifying the space boundaries in relation to what you want, you can start to explore other possibilities. This will require some compromise. The bookcase may still fit the main line using N gauge instead, but you cannot have the detailed locomotives of O gauge. Ask yourself, what is most important to you? Equally, what is least important to you? If your greatest interest is in main line running, then that is what is most important to you. You should therefore choose N gauge (you can always have a few O gauge locomotives for the mantelpiece).

Use the wish list to decide what you can and cannot live without. Put a tick against those things you must have and a cross against those that you can live without. If you cannot decide, ask yourself whether the lack of an item on the list would so diminish your satisfaction with the layout that you would probably not build it at all. Be prepared to make some harsh decisions. Some of the items on the wish list will be a case of 'this one or that one, not both'. By approaching the wish list in a logical manner, and identifying what's vital to you to have,

you will find it easier to make the compromises that all layouts require, without really feeling that you have had to compromise at all.

SELECTIVE COMPRESSION

Real railways are very big. They have lots of space to play with. Model railways, by comparison, are very

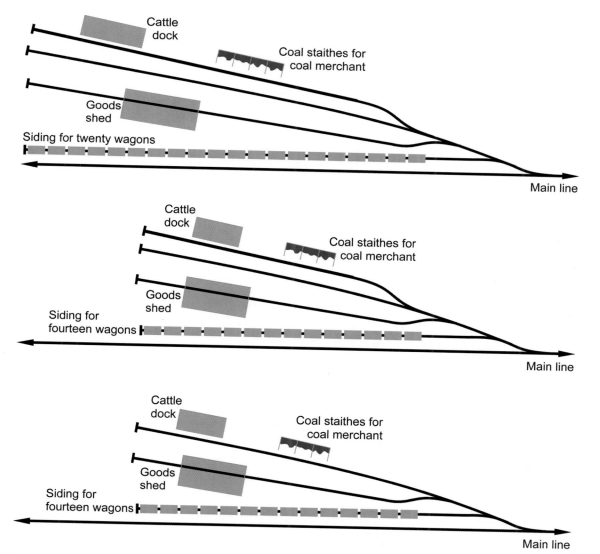

The plan at the top shows a 'real' goods yard as it would be with full-length sidings. The middle plan shows the sidings reduced by one quarter; the goods shed, cattle dock and coal staithes have also been reduced in size. The bottom plan has had one of the sidings removed, yet it is still recognizable as the plan at the top.

small – they only have baseboards. How can you fit the real quart into the modelled pint pot without losing the essence of the prototype? The answer lies with selective compression. You can take a real ten-coach train and have a model that still looks realistic by reducing it to six coaches. But when you design a model railway, it is not just train length that you can reduce. You can compress anything. The trick is to be selective.

Consider a goods yard and for this example let us assume that you want to model a real location. The actual goods yard may have had four sidings – one to a goods shed, one to a cattle dock and coal merchants, and two general-purpose sidings. Each siding may have been capable of holding twenty steam-era wagons. The first thing to consider is reducing the length of the sidings. Including the turnouts, four sidings capable of holding twenty wagons each are going to be very long. If the number of wagons in each siding is halved to ten, the amount of space required along the length of the baseboard will also be halved. This still leaves a theoretical capacity of forty wagons in the station, although this 'full to capacity' figure may make things look too busy.

Next, consider losing one of the four sidings. The goods shed and coal merchants are a feature of virtually every steam-era goods yard, so you cannot do without those. Not all yards had a cattle dock, although, if this is an actual location you are modelling, this may be a key feature. People who knew the location would remember that there was a cattle dock. However, would they notice if you reduce the general sidings from two to one? Many modellers have used these tricks to model an actual location and report that people viewing the layout still recognize the place, despite the changes. You can, of course, stray further from the prototype, especially if you merely wish to base your model on a real place. The key thing is that the selective compression retains the spirit of the type of place you are trying to represent in your model.

There are other areas for compression. If your trains are being reduced in length, the platform length can be reduced as well. If you are modelling a motive power depot, choose a shorter turntable,

as long as it is big enough for the largest engine you may wish to turn. Engine sheds were big buildings, so, like the goods yard example, reduce the number of tracks in the shed and the length of those tracks, which will in turn reduce the footprint of the building.

Even on a room-sized scenic layout, there are opportunities for compression. If you model a viaduct, reduce the number of arches going across the valley. While the height of the viaduct is unlikely to be a space constraint (unless there is something stored under the layout, such as with a bookcase), consider also reducing the height, or else the relative proportions of the structure may not look right.

Selective compression does not mean leaving something out to put something in its place. It allows us to avoid one of the easiest traps to fall into when we are working in less space than we would ideally like to have – that of a natural tendency to try to cram in as much as possible, making the resulting model look cramped and unrealistic. Most real railway locations have an airiness about them due to all the space that they occupy. Not only that, they are set in a real landscape, with no baseboard edges and back scenes to constrain the view of reality. You may choose to compromise on this if you want as much track as possible for operational potential; if you want to shunt wagons, have a busy station and a motive power depot all on one small layout, that's your choice. It will be huge fun to operate, but it will not look as realistic. Use your wish list, identify what you want the most, then apply some selective compression to get a greater feeling of space in the actual space available.

FORCED PERSPECTIVE

It is a simple fact that things in the far distance look smaller, even tiny. Things in the near distance will look smaller, but less noticeably so. In painting terms, this is known as perspective. But the rear of a model railway baseboard is nothing like far distance. Working in a smaller space means that the baseboards may be narrower than we would ideally like. What can the railway modeller do to make the distance seem further away than it is? By adopting a few

Two class 03 shunters with the same type of hopper wagon, but how far apart are they? Actually, they are as close as the length of the locomotive itself. This scene on the OO gauge 'Denshaw Quarry' layout has been staged to illustrate forced perspective. The rear locomotive and wagon are N gauge versions of the front ones, which makes them half the size. The only photographic trick was to reduce the depth of field deliberately so as to make the background and foreground slightly out of focus, as would be the case for a human eye focusing on the front locomotive.

artistic tricks, you can avoid your layout looking like some track on a plank of wood. It is still a plank of wood, but, by fooling the eye, we can make the brain forget the facts and enjoy the illusion thus created. The simplest of these illusions is called forced perspective.

As objects recede further from the eye, they appear to get smaller. If you also make the objects physically smaller as you move them further away, this doubles the perspective effect – in other words, you force the perspective to work twice as hard for the eye. It will not really be noticeable if the hills are made smaller, as landscape varies considerably in size. Tree can be made smaller, although, ironically, it is a generally accepted fact that most trees are already modelled far smaller than they should be. Real trees would tower over real trains; yet, in a model setting, this can look out of proportion even

though it is exactly correct for the scale. Forced perspective works best on manmade objects, as the brain already has some very good information about how they should look when the eye is a prescribed distance away. Make the object smaller and the brain will think that the object is further away. Buildings and road vehicles are the easiest manmade objects to use for forced perspective.

One of the easiest and quickest applications of forced perspective is with buildings, simply by using buildings from the next modelling scale down in size. So if you are modelling in OO gauge, you could use N gauge buildings at the rear of the layout. However, N gauge is half the size of OO gauge, so unless you have several feet of depth to the baseboard, the illusion will not work. The change in scale is too abrupt from foreground to background. It is better to use buildings that are three-quarters of the scale you are working in. In OO gauge, this means constructing buildings to a scale of 3mm to the foot. If you have a corner on a layout, you will have a greater depth into the corner than the main baseboards. Here, you could try buildings in the foreground that are 4mm to the foot, in the middle make them 3mm to the foot, and at the rear 2.5mm, or even 2mm, to the foot, the latter being N gauge. The perspective is gradually narrowing as you look towards the rear.

By working between the main commercial scales for forced perspective, say, between OO gauge and N gauge, there are unlikely to be any commercially available buildings, so it would be necessary to resort to scratch-building (although HO, which is commercially favoured in Europe and America, is a scale of 3.5mm to the foot). However, making buildings from scratch is a lot less demanding than the precision engineering of modelling a steam locomotive – real buildings are rarely perfectly square, so something realistic should be achievable. A slightly easier approach, and a little bit of a cheat, is to buy buildings from one of the many ranges of card kits. These are 'flat-packed', so it is easy to reduce them on a photocopier, or by using a scanner and a computer. These devices allow you to reduce the kit accurately to three-quarters of its original size.

Using buildings for forced perspective is easy in an urban setting, or where you can justify a 'house on the hill', but not all modelling situations are appropriate to using buildings. The next trick is to use road vehicles. It is a common feature to have a road at the rear of the layout, following and eventually crossing the railway. You can make roads narrower at the rear of the layout and alter the length and spacing of white lines, but what about the vehicles themselves? Scratch-building cars is not an easy proposition. There are many ranges of model cars that are made, ironically, with the railway modelling scale in mind first and foremost. You cannot reduce one of these on a photocopier. It is worth looking around outside of the ranges of 'railway cars' for what are toy or collectors' cars. These may be made to a scale that is close to the one you are working in, and, if you are lucky, slightly smaller. The only scale where you

can easily use forced perspective with road vehicles is British N gauge. This is to a scale ratio of 1:148; however, continental N gauge uses the smaller scale ratio of 1:160, and there are several extensive and quality ranges of vehicles available. Admittedly, the steering wheel is on the wrong side, but that is unlikely to be noticeable in the smaller scale.

LOW RELIEF

Any building that is situated at the rear of the layout does not have to be modelled in its entirety – only a part of it will be needed to suggest its presence and purpose. This trick is called 'low-relief' modelling. It is very easy to do, simply a case of cutting a building down the middle as you make it. The bonus is that you can often get two buildings for the price of one.

You do not have to be a student of architecture to understand that most buildings have some key features that identify broadly what they are. Houses and shops are just two storeys and their simple frontage says what they are. Warehouses are taller, with a uniform pattern of large windows and maybe some doors for loading, perhaps with hoists above them. Factories are similar to warehouses, but there may be some pipes, a glazed roof and probably a chimney. The point is that you do not have to model either massive buildings (such as factories) or a succession of smaller buildings (such as a row of houses) in their entirety to know what they are and what their purpose is. In real life, you can only ever see two sides of any building at once, and unless you are looking down on it from a lofty vantage point, you will not get an idea of its actual size. With this concept in mind, you only have to model enough of a building to get sufficient clues as to its purpose. The only question that remains is – how low can you go?

The lowest relief (in reality the thinnest) is to simply create 'cardboard cut-outs' to place against the back scene. These are perhaps little different from just using a back scene with the shapes of buildings painted on. However, they do allow you to add some detail, literally some relief, to the silhouette of a building. You may get away with simply

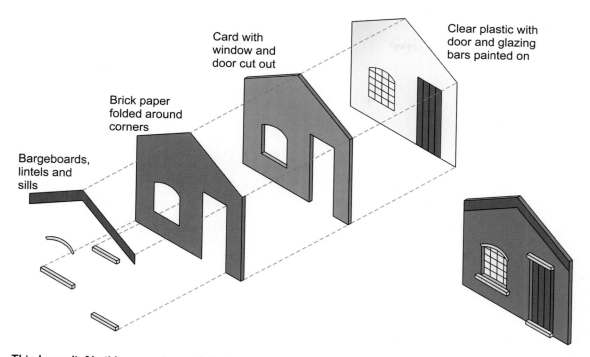

Clear plastic with door and glazing bars painted on

Card with window and door cut out

Brick paper folded around corners

Bargeboards, lintels and sills

Thin low-relief buildings can be made by laminating clear plastic sheet, cardboard and brick paper. This allows details such as lintels, sills and doorsteps to be added, which would otherwise look odd on a building that was just painted on to the back scene. The use of clear plastic means that light will reflect off the windows.

painting a building on to a back scene if you are just representing the end of a row of terraced houses, which is nothing more than a brick wall. Yet if you are modelling windows and doors in the buildings, recessing them and adding doorsteps and window sills will make them look more effective. This can easily be achieved with two layers rather than just one, the inner layer consisting of doors and windows (frames and glazing bars) painted on to thin clear plastic.

Beyond simple silhouette low relief, it is really just a case of how much room you have for the building. Any low-relief building looks fine when viewed directly from the front. The problems can arise when it is viewed from an angle, since the side walls stop abruptly when they reach the back scene. Very thin low-relief buildings, especially tall ones, can look a bit odd just projecting such a short way out of the back scene. The trick is to try to hide the gap between buildings on the back scene. Try using trees between

houses and other structures such as a chimney or a water tower for factories.

Most buildings have a simple sloping roof with an apex down the middle. You can position your building so that the apex is to the front of the layout. The resulting triangle at the top of the building means that the building can be quite shallow, thus saving a lot of space. The downside is that the roof tiles disappear into the back scene, meaning that it may look like it has been chopped in half. Turning the building through 90 degrees means that one whole side of the roof is displayed. This does benefit by showing the roof all the way up to the ridge, which can mean that the building still requires a fair amount of depth. As a roof slopes down the other side of the ridge, the roof cannot be seen anyway, so why model it? However, if you do not model up to the ridge, the building does look like it's been chopped in half. Try not to mix the two orientations of the building described here. The

Differing roof styles for low-relief buildings. The flat-roof building on the left has a parapet that hides the roof. The low building in the middle has two gable ends facing the layout, which accentuates the fact that they are low against the back scene. The larger building on the right has the sloped roof modelled up to the ridge tiles; only by moving around to the left can you see that the end of the building disappears into the sky.

trick is to keep things simple with low-relief build-ings – the aim is that they should blend into the background rather than leap out with architectural complexity.

BACK SCENES

You cannot avoid having a rear to your layout, no matter how much forced perspective you employ. Having a back scene hides the wall or room behind and helps to maintain the illusion that the modeller is seeking to create. The easiest back scene is simply a representation of the sky. This works well in a rural scene, possibly with the hills rising to the rear of the layout. However, it can fail to convince in a more urban setting, if clear blue sky can be glimpsed between the buildings when there should be other buildings instead.

If you are a reasonable artist, you can paint your own back scene. You can employ forced perspec-tive again. Paint the buildings on the back scene but proportionally reduced in size to suggest that they are in the distance. Try continuing roads from the front to the rear of the layout, gradually narrowing the road on the baseboard and continuing to narrow it as you paint it on to the back scene. Be aware, though, that this is a very difficult trick to pull off convincingly. Sometimes, it only looks right when looking straight at it; as you move to either side it fails to convince.

OPPOSITE: *The N Gauge Society Chester Area Group's layout 'Cragmill' has a painted back scene showing a mix of rolling hills and sky. Note how trees and foliage have been planted between the road at the rear and the back scene itself; this softens what would otherwise be an abrupt meeting between the layout and the back scene.*

Trevor Webster's N gauge layout 'Parnhams's Maltings' uses a photographic back scene. A hedge at the back of the road has been used to disguise where the back scene meets the layout.

Some modellers build dioramas (small non-working scenes) and photograph them outside using Mother Nature as a natural back scene. The next best thing for an indoor layout is a photograph of Mother Nature. Painted back scenes on thin paper have been in existence for years; however, realistic photographic back scenes are now available and becoming increasingly popular. If you are handy with digital photography and a computer, you can soon create your own.

Photographic back scenes can work very well, but they can sometimes be too realistic. Digital photography and printing allow for the presentation of a phenomenal level of detail, which is where the problem can lie, since it is often hard to model an equivalent level of detail in the foreground. This inconsistency means that you are looking at two very different levels of presentation, which will make the back scene stand out when you really want it to blend in. A painted back scene, even if you are no artist, can be made to look a little more 'impressionist' – a 'soft and fuzzy' background is less noticeable. It is out of focus, which tricks the eye into thinking it is further away than it really is. A pin-sharp digital image will not achieve that trick. Despite all this caution, there are some very good 'generic' photo back scenes available at reasonable prices and they are well worth a look.

Finally, there is one back scene trap for the unwary to avoid, which is actually nothing to do with the back scene itself. Try not to put tall structures like trees and telegraph poles too close to the rear of the layout, since, depending on your lighting, they can cast shadows on to the back scene. You might get away with a tree casting a shadow on to a hill, but real trees certainly do not cast shadows on the real sky.

This N gauge layout has been deliberately lit with a strong side light to emphasize how the chimney casts a shadow because it is too close to the back scene. The more usual even lighting from above will still cast a slight shadow on the plain sky back scene. A better alternative would have been to site the chimney in front of the adjacent building.

EXIT STAGE LEFT

If your layout design involves any kind of fiddle yard, you are going to have to deal with the transition from your layout to the 'rest of the railway network' that the fiddle yard represents. It is rarely a gradual transition and usually more of an abrupt change from a fully scenic environment to bare baseboards, with lots of storage and rolling stock. It rather spoils any illusion that the model may portray if you watch the train travel from the modelled world of the layout to the completely artificial one of the fiddle yard. From the audience point of view in the theatre, when the actors exit stage left, they cannot be seen suddenly standing behind the scenes. In the same way, your

model trains need to exit the stage to the fiddle yard behind the scenes. There are two basic approaches to this – the rabbit hole and the view blocker.

INTO THE RABBIT HOLE

There are three ways of going to and from the fiddle yard that consist of going into something – bridges, tunnels and buildings. Tunnels are a classic stage exit and they really are a rabbit hole, yet they still need to be constructed with caution. A tunnel portal is usually a bit taller than the height of a bridge and when there is no train moving through it, it has the potential to look like nothing more than a large hole in the back scene that separates the layout from the fiddle yard. You expect tunnels to be portals of Stygian gloom, not to show the bright lights of the fiddle yard behind.

The Warrington Model Railway Club's OO9 layout 'Dienw' has some well-modelled tunnels. Note how the tunnel lining is modelled into the tunnel and that tracks disappear convincingly into the gloom with no sign of the fiddle yard on the other side. Finally, there is sufficient landscape above to convince that the railway really disappears into the hill.

A simple tunnel mouth hard up against the back scene will look as unrealistic on the layout as the fiddle yard that can be viewed through it.

Most tunnels are approached in a cutting, so by modelling this and a little of the land over the tunnel mouth, you will create more of an impression of the train disappearing into a tunnel and not a stage exit. A further vital trick for the illusion to work is to model some of the tunnel bore itself. By giving the first few inches of the inside of the tunnel a wall, preferably painted black, you literally create 'tunnel vision' so that the fiddle yard on the other side cannot be seen. Even if you are restricted in the amount of landscape on the layout for the tunnel, try to include this feature at the start of the fiddle yard itself.

The real builders of railways tried to avoid tunnels as they are a costly construction enterprise, so the most common stage exit is the bridge over the railway lines. A bridge without a deck looks a little odd, so it is necessary to model the bridge in its entirety. The model bridge usually carries a road (with an assortment of cars, carts, buses and so on, though don't overdo it), or it can take a canal or even more railway lines (which of necessity will never see a train running over them).

The bridge parapet next to the fiddle yard can be modelled right up against the back scene if space is really at a premium and painting the back scene a simple sky colour gives a reasonable result. It is better, though, if the bridge can be brought forwards a little. In this case, the back scene goes all

These fully modelled bridges on the Warrington Model Railway Club's N gauge layout 'Glazebrook' cover diverging double tracks as they disappear into the fiddle yard just beyond. The back scene has been curved to follow the direction of the road, with holes cut in at the bottom to allow the trains through.

the way down to ground level with a hole cut into it that is just big enough to take a train. Some bridges offered quite tight clearances at the side and were no taller than was necessary to clear the gauge of the railway (gauge in this case not referring to the width between the rails, but all the crucial dimensions to avoid the rolling stock hitting the line-side infrastructure). Combining this with the average width of a road bridge (enough for two lanes of traffic) provides the same effect as a tunnel. With the hole in the back scene being smaller than required for a tunnel, there is less chance of seeing the fiddle yard beyond.

The final type of rabbit hole is to exit through a building. Obviously, this is not going to suit most situations, as few stations were ever reached by running through a building (though the combination of a station building atop a road bridge does provide a very effective exit if you only want to model part of the platform length). However, in any kind of industrial situation from a dockyard to a factory, it would be quite common to run through one building to access another part of the site. As these 'doorway' openings might just be large enough to accept rolling stock, they offer a means of having a small hole through which to reach the fiddle yard. Buildings can be used as miniature fiddle yards besides the main fiddle yard, for example modelling part of a large goods shed into which wagons can be shunted and then swapped over.

ABOVE: *On the OO gauge layout 'Denshaw Quarry', the fiddle yard is housed in a large industrial building into which this train of hoppers can be seen entering through a doorway.*

BELOW: *Once the train is in the fiddle yard, the door is closed and all fiddling activity is hidden from the viewer. Note also how, from certain angles, the water tower will act as a view blocker so that you cannot see into the fiddle yard when the door is open.*

On the N gauge layout 'Mill Lane Sidings', the fiddle yard is a single track within the large building that can be seen at the top right. To get there, it passes through a narrow gap between two smaller buildings. These are joined by an overbridge carrying some pipes, which blocks the view of the track from above the buildings. The final view blocker is the deliberate placement of the water tank, which hides the fiddle yard entrance from even the acutest of angles.

VIEW BLOCKERS

What options do you have when modelling a place that's fairly flat, where level crossings are used instead of bridges and tunnels are unheard of? In this case, the railway will have to disappear into a hole in the back scene that divides the layout from the fiddle yard. This hole can be made as small as possible to avoid seeing much of the fiddle yard (just enough to clear the widest and tallest rolling stock). A train that disappears (literally) into a blue sky can destroy the illusion created by the layout. You can get away with it to some extent on very long layouts as attention can be focused elsewhere, or you may be standing some way away from the 'hole in the sky'. On shorter layouts, it will not work. So to avoid

seeing the hole in the sky, the answer is simple – just hide it.

To hide the hole, use a view blocker. We have a tendency to design layouts with buildings at the back and trains at the front. As railway enthusiasts, we do not want to hide the trains any more than we need to. However, at the extremes of the layout where the fiddle yards are, if a few scenic elements are brought to the foreground, the view of the hole in the back scene can be obscured. Very often, all it takes is one building at the front to do this.

A lot depends on how long your layout is and thus how far away from the fiddle yard your viewing point may be. As you design your layout, if you think that there will be a point from where you will regularly be able to see the train disappear into the hole, design

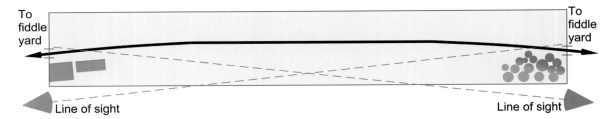

To fiddle yard

To fiddle yard

Line of sight

Line of sight

On this plan, buildings are used on the left to hide the exit through the back scene to the fiddle yard, while trees are used for the same purpose on the right. The red dashed lines show the most acute line of vision that is possible from each end and that it is not possible to see the hole in the back scene. The main line has been curved slightly at each end so that fewer buildings and trees are needed.

in another view blocker. Also consider curving the track as it enters the fiddle yard, as this will enhance the effect of 'disappearing' behind a building.

If there are no buildings suitable for a rural scene that you may be modelling, try using trees. These can be 'planted' anywhere, as densely as necessary. Real trees are often surprisingly tall things, so you can get a lot of height to your view blocker without needing to model a skyscraper.

CHAPTER FIVE

LEVELS, LAYERS AND SHELVES

Wouldn't it be great if there was a way to double the space at our disposal? No matter whether we have access to just one wall of a room or all of the room, we would all like twice as much railway as we think that we have actual space for. We tend to think of baseboards in two dimensions – length and depth combined to give available surface area. Yet if you think in three dimensions, you can have more – twice as much more. It is not strictly a third dimension, as that relates to the height of what is on the baseboard – buildings, trees, hills and so on. If you go up above your layout (or even down below), it is more like a fourth dimension, as you are putting one part of your layout above another. Just like Doctor Who's TARDIS, your layout can be made to appear bigger on the inside than it is on the outside.

Building a normal single-level layout is within the grasp of most modellers. Adding another level means deviating from the norm, with all the additional challenges that a traditional baseboard does not present. When you consider what the concepts of multilevel design can deliver, in terms of increased scenic and operational potential within a given space, you may well conclude that the traditional flat baseboard is a very old-fashioned way of doing things.

LAYERS OF TERMINOLOGY

Before we set foot into this newly realized 'fourth dimension', it is worth broadly defining our terminology. There are no globally accepted definitions, so, as usual, they differ depending on which side of

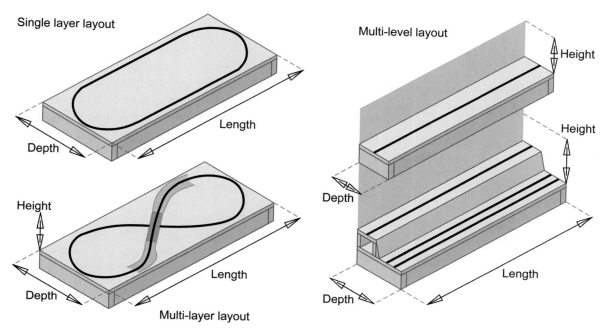

A single-layer baseboard need only be measured in terms of length and depth. A figure-of-eight layout additionally needs to be measured in terms of height, since the track crosses itself by means of a bridge with inclines either side; this is now a multilayer layout. A multilevel layout is a series of shelves above each other. Note that in this example, the lower level has one track higher than the others, making it a multilayer level.

the Atlantic you are. Therefore, the terms used in this book will be defined before we get lost in a confusion of layers, levels and decks.

The main distinction to be made here is between a multilayer layout and a multilevel layout. A multilayer layout is one with a traditional single baseboard on which there are multiple layers of track. A classic example of this would be a figure-of-eight where the track rises to a higher layer to cross itself. In this case, everything is just three-dimensional. In contrast, a multilevel layout exploits the 'fourth dimension' by placing one part of the layout completely and separately above the other. Think of the shelves in a bookcase, how they are stacked above each other (American modellers refer to multilevel layouts as 'multideck' layouts – think of the decks on a ship). The key part of a multilevel layout is that the levels are separate, therefore independent. In the multilayer example of the figure-of-eight layout, one track crosses over the other by means of an integrated scenic feature, usually a bridge. The tracks on each level of a multilevel layout are above each other, but they are not linked scenically.

Although the levels of a multilevel layout are separated from each other in a scenic context, they are not separated from an operational point of view. After all, we want to make our layout twice as big as it might be, not build two different layouts one above the other (although, if you cannot make up your mind what to model, there's nothing wrong with two layouts, and most of this chapter will still be pertinent to achieving that goal). The challenge, then, is how to get our train from one level to another. Fortunately, there are plenty of solutions on offer, from the complexity of a helix or train lift, to the simplicity of a gradient or cassette system.

Finally, the analogy was used above of shelves in a bookcase when introducing the idea of a multilevel layout, which brings us on to what are termed 'shelf layouts'. A shelf layout sits on a shelf – it is as simple as that. You can think of it as a single-level version of the multilevel layout by using just the one shelf, or as a true multilevel layout consisting of several shelves. At first glance, there seems little difference between a shelf layout and a multilevel layout beyond the

obvious of the depth of the baseboards. This is true enough, so shelf layouts (even single-level ones) have been included in this chapter on multilevel layouts because they have sufficient in common that it makes for a logical grouping.

MULTILAYER LAYOUTS

Do you have enough baseboard to have the model railway that you want using just one layer? Consider whether an extra layer would broaden your horizons by extending the scenic and operational possibilities. By putting some of the track over other track, this increases the amount that can be placed in the same three-dimensional space. Think of it as folding or bending a much larger single-layer design in and over itself. This means that some of the tracks will need to be covered and thus out of view, but as long as you can access this track for cleaning and any derailments, it is not an issue.

The first and most obvious thing to cover up is the fiddle yard. Some modellers consider that the fiddle yard is a bit of a waste of space, even though it does the vital job of holding all your trains and representing the 'rest of the railway network'. By placing the fiddle yard underneath one of the main layout boards, the space that the fiddle yard would have occupied can be used to build, for example, another station. Most of the fiddle yard solutions can be made to work under an existing baseboard. The main thing to consider is how easy it will be to access the fiddle yard, both from the point of view of getting the trains down there and in terms of getting your hands in there as well. There is no escaping the need to be able to reach inside this subterranean fiddle yard. No matter how good your track and operation, you can bet that there will be a derailment down there at some point in the future.

While a fiddle yard under the baseboard is conveniently out of the way, heading down to it is a little trickier when building the baseboards. The easier approach, and the one that most modellers take, is to keep the fiddle yard on the same level as the other baseboards and to go up to another

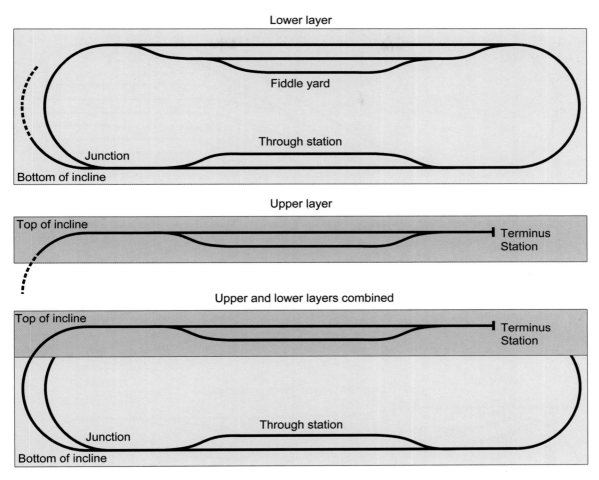

The lower layer is a standard oval layout with a station on one side and a fiddle yard on the other. The upper layer is a simple terminus layout. Combining the upper and lower layers gives two layouts in one, as well as hiding the fiddle yard and making use of the space that it must necessarily occupy. A junction and an incline are all that are needed to join the two layers.

layer of the layout that sits over the fiddle yard. This simple approach creates perhaps one of the most flexible layout designs of all. At the datum layer there can be a continuous loop (probably double track) with a through station on one side and the fiddle yard on the other – ideal for those times when you want to just sit and watch the trains go by. On the higher layer, a terminus station can be added. Joining the two levels will require a gradient (probably a single track) and, where they meet, a junction arrangement. That's a lot of railway in a small space.

Convention tends to dictate a terminus station up above simply because it only needs one gradient up to it – a through station would mean having to come down on the other side, which is fine, of course, if you have the room. A terminus station gives you the greater operational challenges of terminating trains, such as running round. Even in a modest room-sized space, the chances are that there will not be acres of space above the fiddle yard to model a huge station, so the design principles elsewhere in this book for creating a modest station in a small space are still applicable. The space over the fiddle yard does not

Lower layer

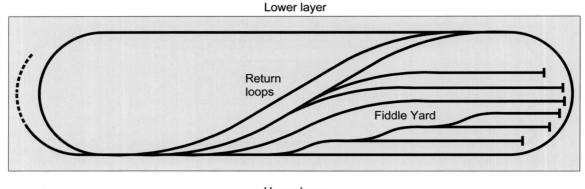

Upper layer

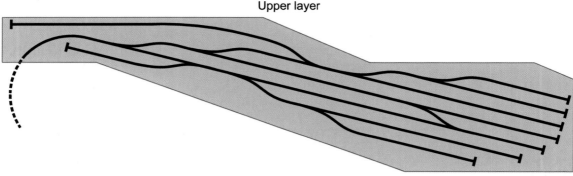

Upper and lower layers combined

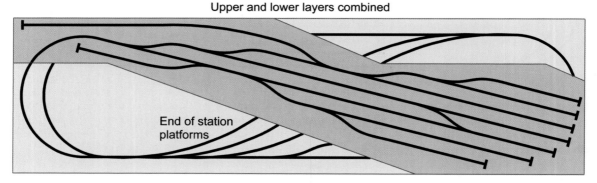

This is a tabletop design for N gauge that allows the upper level to be placed at a diagonal to create a much larger terminus. Most of the fiddle yard consists of sidings that are reached from the bottom right corner under the terminus. There is no room for a station on the lower level; however, where the four tracks at the front enter the reverse loops and the fiddle yard, these can represent the end of the platforms of a larger station. The upper level provides a frontage to this lower 'station', which could be disguised with the front of a large station roof.

have to be a terminus station; it can be whatever you want it to be, such as a motive power depot, or a goods yard.

Do not imagine that this design of a terminus station over a fiddle yard is the preserve of room-sized layouts. If you step down a scale to N gauge, it is quite feasible to fit it all into a tabletop layout. Believe it or not, this actually gives even more possibilities, as track can be placed over the middle part of the oval, which on a room-sized layout would have

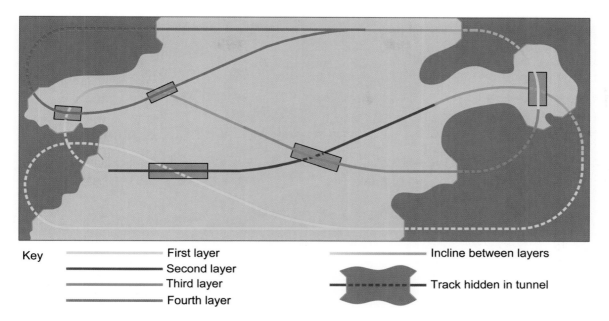

Key

First layer
Second layer
Third layer
Fourth layer

Incline between layers
Track hidden in tunnel

This basic plan shows the 'rabbit warren' style of layout suitable for prototype railways from mountainous places such as the Swiss Alps and some narrow gauge railways. The track crosses over itself five times as it climbs from a reverse loop at the front to one at the back, which means that there are four layers. Tunnels are used to disguise the reverse loops on the first and fourth layers, as well as most of the curves that loop the track back on itself. The plan offers twice the length of track as would be possible with a single-layer oval in the same space.

to remain clear in order to give you actual space in which to sit. So instead of the upper-layer terminus being parallel with the baseboard and over the fiddle yard, it can be placed at a diagonal. The diagonal will give you fractionally longer platforms and certainly more room to 'fan out' either side. Of course, this comes at the expense of the amount of visible running tracks below. However, by adding in a diagonal that crosses the lower-level loop, you have the chance to turn the direction of trains as well as watching them loop the loop. This is a very powerful device indeed as it means that trains can leave your terminus, make as many trips round the loop as you desire, then reverse direction so that they come back up the gradient and terminate in the station. Truly, your train has been somewhere and come back again.

There is no theoretical limit to the number of layers that can be added to your layout, although eventually you would reach the ceiling. Layouts set

in the Swiss mountains are well known for constantly looping back and crossing over themselves multiple times, while popping in and out of tunnels. Such layouts are prototypical and three or even four layers are quite possible, with the same track as one long loop from the bottom to the top. The trick here is to consider train lengths in relation to the track plan. You want to avoid the rear coach of a train disappearing into a tunnel at the same time as the locomotive appears from another if both can be viewed from the same angle, which would happen where the train loops back on itself. If the train disappears from one layer completely and reappears on the next, there is less of a realization that it is the same train going backwards and forwards up the layout, even though it crosses the same scene several times on its journey.

These complex mountainous track plans are often referred to as 'rabbit warren' layouts for obvious reasons. Such designs can lead to cramped

baseboards with too much track, even if it is broken up into separate scenes by tunnels and bridges, unless that's what you want. However, no one can deny that the end result is an impressive three-dimensional model of potentially towering height. The height of the layout may mean that a permanent site is the only practical proposition.

If you want a multilayer layout that is a little smaller, but no less ambitious in scope, consider a narrow gauge subject. The 'rabbit warren' approach is just as popular in a mountainous Welsh setting as it is in a Swiss one. Certainly, if you have ever had a ride on the Ffestiniog Railway from Porthmadog to Ffestiniog itself, you will know that it twists and turns, hugs steep hillsides and climbs an incredible height. It even loops and crosses over itself at Dduallt – there's always a prototype for everything.

Scenic layouts snaking through the landscape have no choice but to double back and cross over themselves in order to gain height. Having the train pass through the same scene more than once, even if it is heading in the opposite direction, may be considered unrealistic. Therefore, some modellers may be a little cool towards the 'rabbit warren' type of layout, but they suit the prototypes that they support and are the ultimate realization of the multilayer design. The polar opposite of the 'rabbit warren', indeed the opposite of the multilayer-layout concept, is to ensure that the railway only passes through the same scene once, as real railways do. If that is what you want, but do not have the available area for it, you will need to go up a whole new level.

You can still have multilayer layouts with absolutely no attempt to join the two layers. A popular approach with micro-layouts is to put a station on the

higher level at the rear of the layout, with a yard or motive power depot at the front on the lower level. The fiddle yard for the lower level can be underneath the station on the higher level. Alternatively, consider mixing gauges, with standard gauge on the lower level and a narrow gauge industrial railway on the upper level. Mix and match to your heart's content.

SINGLE-LEVEL LAYOUTS – ON A SHELF

You would be forgiven for thinking that shelves are just for books and ornaments. For the railway modeller who must be economical with the space available, and possibly share that space with everyone else, the shelf layout offers a lot of possibilities that should be given serious consideration. A shelf layout for the modeller with restrictions on space will help in one of two ways. The first is where a permanent layout is desired, but the space has to be shared with another use – the shelf layout can 'float' above whatever else is in the room. The second way a shelf layout can help is by going up another level above the layout – the multilevel approach.

Don't just limit yourself to a shelf that is wide enough to hold a book. A shelf layout can still occupy a depth up to 18in (0.46m), even 2ft (0.6m) at a push. This gives plenty of room for associated railway items alongside the main line, such as stations, goods yards and factories.

One way of sharing a space such as a spare room with another use for that room is to put the model railway layout above everything else. With a traditional baseboard that rests on legs or trestles, you are limited to not much more than tabletop height. A layout at chest height is possible, though it tends to be the domain of exhibition layouts that are presented in this way to put the layout closer to eye level. This saves the viewer having to stoop down to see the layout, or otherwise view it 'from the air', what is sometimes referred to as the 'helicopter view'. Seen at eye level, any lack of depth on a layout will be less obvious than if it were to be viewed from above. If a normal chair is too low for the shelf

OPPOSITE: *This view of Stephen Farmer's multilayer N gauge layout 'Wulstanton Road' clearly shows a station on the upper layer and a goods yard on the lower layer. Each layer has its own fiddle yard and there is no connection between them. Besides having greater visual interest, where a layout has significant depth, raising the rear section to another layer can improve the visibility of the details that are furthest away from the viewer.*

ABOVE: *This view of the N gauge North American layout '37th Street' is taken at eye level and deliberately includes the edge of the baseboard and the top of the back scene to frame the image. The depth is just 12in (0.3m), yet from this angle there is a feeling of space and distance.*

BELOW: *This is the same view of '37th Street', but having stood up to give the more traditional 'helicopter view'. It is now easier to see the detail of the track plan, which is helpful for operation; however, the limit of the depth of the layout is now all too plain to see. You will always see the front edge of a layout, but making the rear limit of the layout easier to see only accentuates the fact that this is a layout on a shelf.*

layout, consider purchasing an inexpensive bar stool to gain extra height.

What the space under the shelf is used for is up to you (or the rest of the occupiers of the house). You can store a bed on its side and with a few pieces of other typical bedroom furniture, easily convert the room into a guest room; as the layout is up in the air, your guests will still be quite comfortable. In the age of the computer and, indeed, home-working for many of us, the spare room is often used as a study or office. You might not be able to use the room for both functions at the same time, but, once again, there is a simple and quick shift that is possible between the disparate uses of the room. The only thing to watch for is the depth of furniture under the shelf layout. You do not want to find yourself having to reach over, say, a desk with a computer on it, in order to uncouple a locomotive from a train. If such a situation is likely, be aware of where any bulky furniture will be within a room when designing your track plan. Also, consider where the furniture will go before you build the layout, so that the two uses of the room are complementary. For example, you cannot run a shelf layout at chest height across a window, so the desk can be placed there.

A shelf layout is a single-level version of a multilevel layout. Many of the design, build and presentation considerations for multilevel layouts apply equally to shelf layouts.

MULTILEVEL LAYOUTS

When initially planning your model railway, it is hard to consider anything other than a traditional baseboard – a flat top with legs. There are variations and different ways it can be constructed, but, ultimately, thousands of modellers have made a flat top with legs. Then they have run out of space. The greater the depth of the baseboard, the greater the scenic possibilities for rolling hills or urban sprawl through which the railway can realistically wind itself. Yet there is only so much space in a room before the railway loops back on itself and you run out of space. The solution is incredibly simple. Look at your traditional baseboard and ask yourself where there is

a load of extra space to be had. The answer is right there in front of you. All you have to do is just look up above the baseboard.

Multilevel layouts have become increasingly popular in North American railway modelling (or 'model railroading', as they say across the pond) and there is a good reason for this. At one time, the tradition for American layouts was very much towards a focus on the scenic masterpiece, with less attention on operation, which could be troublesome by being prone to derailments, stalling and phantom uncoupling, problems that have beset us all in the past. There are plenty of American modellers who are capable of building substantial layouts with brilliant scenery; however, there is one thing that this group of modellers is now particularly interested in, and that is operation. American modellers really strive to build something that can be operated as close as possible to the real railway. The problem is that real railways, as we know, are very long things, so if you want a decent run with a few stations on the way, you need a lot of length. So ask yourself, do you want to build a layout just to look at, or do you want to operate it as well?

Consider if you were to slice the traditional 4ft × 2ft (1.2m × 0.6m) baseboard down the middle. If you take one 4ft × 1ft (1.2m × 0.3m) slice and place it above the other, you could double the length of running line at your disposal. If your focus is on operation, the philosophy goes that it is not necessary to see, or indeed model, much beyond the immediate boundaries of the railway itself. If you limit your vision to the relatively narrow strip of land that a few main-line tracks will occupy, just a narrow strip of baseboard will be required. In other words, all you need is a shelf. The American multilevel layout concept is very much about getting a longer railway in the space that is available. A longer railway means more stations and factories to serve, which increases the operational complexity and thus the enjoyment.

Many of these American multilevel layouts still occupy a large basement or attic and are truly massive; however, we can take the ideas and use them to exploit the more modest spaces that are at the core of this book. The principle is still the same

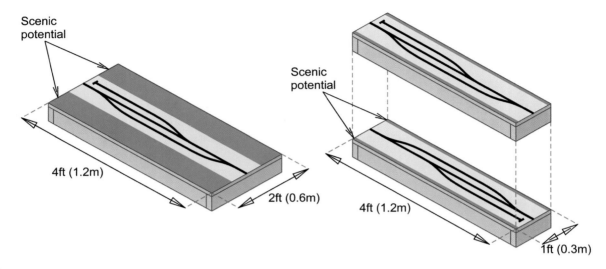

Scenic
potential

Scenic
potential

4ft (1.2m)

2ft (0.6m)

4ft (1.2m)

1ft (0.3m)

A multilevel layout will give increased operating potential by having twice as much track. By converting one deep baseboard into two narrow baseboards one above the other, it is possible to get twice as much main line for the same surface area. However, the trade-off is a much reduced scenic potential.

– no matter what space you have, if you add another level, you can double the length of the railway. You can even triple it if you go so far as to add a third level.

Such a radical new direction for layout design will immediately throw up a few questions. How do you build it? What about lighting? How do you sit down to two different levels? So let's take a practical look at some of the challenges involved in going up as well as around a room.

First of all, and perhaps the most fundamental possible objection, is that you may think that an upper level, hanging over the layout below, is going to spoil any illusion of reality that you are trying to create. The sky from the lower level goes up and meets not the heavens, but another baseboard. As real as any layout may appear to be, it is still an illusion. Remember that the advantage of another level is to have twice as much layout. It's our old friend compromise again – you trade off a little bit of the illusion in order to maximize operating potential. Yet once you start to focus on actually operating the trains and concentrate on moving trains, shunting and uncoupling, your brain starts to lose focus on the surroundings. You will soon stop noticing that there

is another level above you or that the back scene is only a short distance away.

How high should the upper level be above the lower lever? If you want a lot of sky, or anything tall such as trees, buildings or hills, the upper level needs to be set at a height that will accommodate those things required on the lower level. If you want to model an urban environment with skyscrapers, quite a large gap will be needed between the levels. Even a rural landscape can require a similar degree of separation if the scene is going to be framed with a few mountains at the back. Ultimately, it's a matter of personal taste with a dash of the practical (how you are to view each level). It is something that is hard to visualize as the end product, but, if a mistake is made, it is difficult to change once the levels are built and installed. If you have access to some adjustable shelves in the house or garage, take the time to borrow them and mock up a few scenes to see how they will look at different heights, and with different distances between the two levels. This will also help to answer the next question – how high should the levels be off the floor?

You may prefer to operate your layout from a chair, which is fine for the lower level, but less so

These shelves are from the ever versatile 'Ivar' system from Ikea (the holes visible in the rear posts are the increments of adjustment for the shelves). The photo is taken so that the top shelf is at eye level when standing (the highest practical limit for a shelf layout). Placing items of rolling stock (in this case OO gauge) on the shelves makes it easy to work out comfortable operating heights and viewing angles.

for the upper level unless you have some taller bar stools. Or you could just stand in order to operate the upper level. As multilevel layouts enable more intensive operation over a longer space, the chances are that you will be following a train from one part of the layout to another, say from the fiddle yard all the way to a terminus station, perhaps shunting some sidings along the way. It is therefore more convenient to be on your feet than sat in a chair for this kind of 'hands-on' operation. So it does not matter that the layout is on a shelf at chest height. You get a brilliant eye-level view of the trains moving through your layout, plus rolling stock is within easy reach if using manual uncoupling.

Choose the height that is the most comfortable for you. Remember that lower baseboards (in relation to your eye level) mean bending your head more to see the layout. Go to a model railway exhibition and you will find layouts at all sorts of different heights. See which one is the most comfortable for you to view when standing up. The higher the levels from the floor, the closer they can be together. The viewing angle between them is reduced, so the closer the eye is in relation to them.

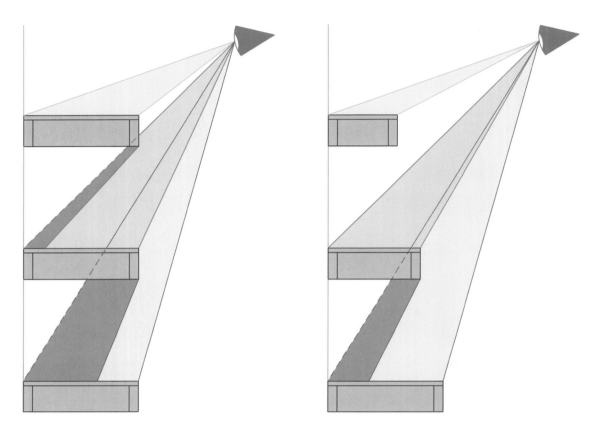

Here are three levels of a multilevel layout and it is assumed that the operator is standing so that the top level is just below eye level. On the left, the baseboards are the same depth for each level – part of the middle level and two-thirds of the bottom level are obscured. On the right, the baseboard depth is progressively reduced with each level, so that the middle level is fully visible and the bottom layer is only partially obscured. Adjusting the height between levels will also affect how much can be seen, while operating the bottom level from a sitting position would make it fully visible.

Do not be tied to a control panel as if you were stuck in a signal box (unless that's what you want), but get out there with your train and travel around the layout with it. You can do this with analogue control, although there is no doubting that DCC offers greater flexibility, with the ability to unplug a controller from one point and plug it in further down the line without having to stop the train.

Having determined heights, let us look at depth. How deep should each level be? Again, it is a matter of personal taste regarding what you want to put on each level. You can get a surprising amount of track into a mere 1ft (0.3m) depth from OO gauge downwards. A level can be deeper, though be careful

of going much beyond 2ft (0.6m), as things could start to get a bit heavy for a shelf. Whatever your depth, if you are going to place the level on brackets attached to the walls, make sure that you screw into the wood framing of any kind of stud wall – the last thing you want is for the upper level to fall on to the level below, destroying two layouts in one go.

Do the levels have to be the same depth? Once again, there are no hard and fast rules, though a lower level can be deeper, especially if it rests on a traditional four legs and flat-top structure. The lower level can have a more complex station and yard, while the upper, narrower level, may support a branch line or a terminus station. Be wary of making

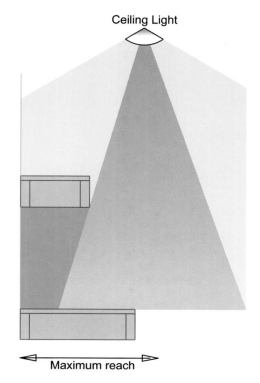
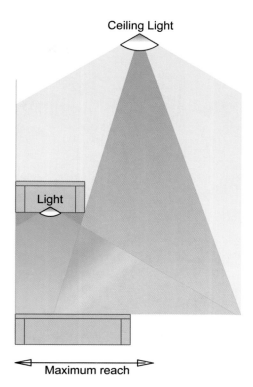

Be aware of what your maximum reach is such that you can easily access the back of the upper level. The diagram on the left shows that by only using a ceiling light, the upper level will cast a shadow on to the lower level. Adding a light underneath the upper level, as shown in the diagram on the right, will remove any shadows. This is a good idea anyway as your own body will also cast a shadow if you only rely on a ceiling light.

the lower level so deep that you cannot easily reach across it to the back of the upper level.

You may think that an upper level will cast a shadow over the lower level. The opposite can be true if you fit lighting under the upper level to illuminate the level below. As an aside, whatever type of layout you build, no matter how big or small, it will benefit from good lighting. Take a look at exhibition layouts with a pelmet over the entire layout and see how much better it looks being able to see all the detail. Do not rely on room lighting alone, as you will cast your own shadow over the layout. Therefore, if you build a layout at home and fit lighting above it, why not build a layout on top of the lighting? You can put lights over the upper level as well, so that everything is well lit. There are many lighting solutions on offer, too many to list here, but simple strip lighting is easy and cost-effective. As with any mains wiring, if you are not sure how to do it, get a man who can – a qualified electrician is a small price to pay for peace of mind.

A neat solution is to build independent legs that support all three layers of a multilevel-type layout – the lower level, the upper level and the lighting at the top (though you may consider the last to be an optional extra). These legs can be joined together for rigidity by bolting the baseboards to them. This offers a 'portable permanent' layout solution that can be easily disassembled to allow work to be done to the room, or for a house move.

Consider also adding facias to all the levels to hide lights, wires, turnout motors and so on. By painting

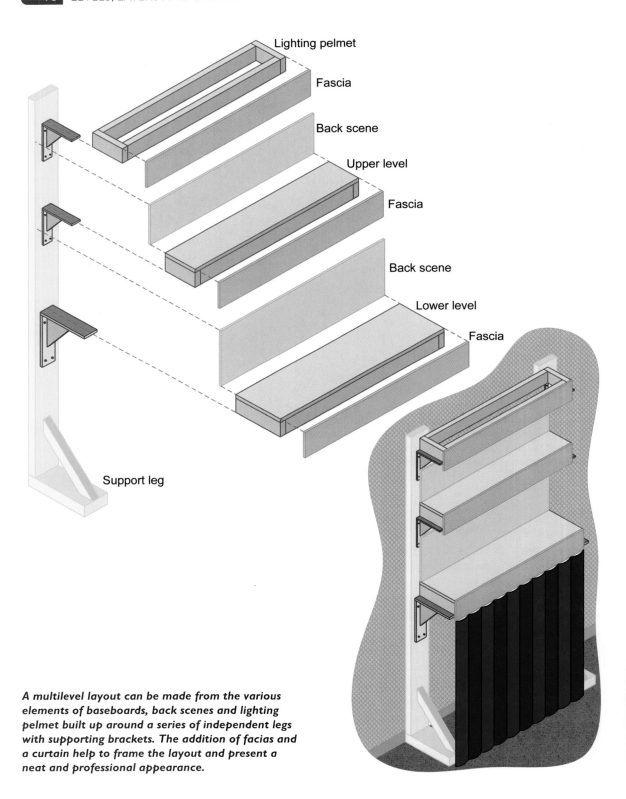

Lighting pelmet

Fascia

Back scene

Upper level

Fascia

Back scene

Lower level

Fascia

Support leg

A multilevel layout can be made from the various elements of baseboards, back scenes and lighting pelmet built up around a series of independent legs with supporting brackets. The addition of facias and a curtain help to frame the layout and present a neat and professional appearance.

them a neutral colour, they will not distract the eye from the contents of the layout – after a few minutes of operation, you will forget that they are there at all. The facia on the top level helps to frame the lower level so that you do not see where the sky ends. It makes for a picture frame, even to the extent of adding sides where the layout moves from one scene to another.

If you plan on having a friend round to help you operate your multilevel layout, avoid locating a station on the upper level directly above a station on the lower level. This avoids having two operators being in the same place at the same time, both getting in each other's way as they try to operate their respective station.

GOING UP (AND DOWN) FROM ONE LEVEL TO ANOTHER

Having a multilevel layout does not mean having to have two independent layouts that never meet, as there are several solutions to bring the two levels together. They differ in how much space they require. The whole objective of a multilevel layout is to increase the operational space, so it is a bit pointless if the space required to move between the levels negates the space gained by having another level. They also differ in complexity – a safe and reliable means of swapping trains between levels is required. Basically, they fall into two categories – those where the train drives itself between levels and those where something else moves the train between levels. Each has its advantages and disadvantages.

If you choose a solution from the first category, whereby the train drives itself between levels, then a little bit of mathematics will be required in order to work out how far the train needs to travel in order to get the desired 'lift'. This is what gradients (in other words, inclines) are all about. The old way of measuring gradients was 'x in y', so a one in ten gradient means going ten units along to gain one unit of height. Therefore to gain 1in in height, it is necessary to go 10in along. So if you need to gain 10in, the requirement is 100in along. The new way of measuring gradients that can be seen on road signs now is as a percentage, but 10 per cent is just the same as one in ten. Before any mathematics, you need to determine the maximum gradient that your model trains can handle, and for this, you need a simple test track.

You can quickly set up a plank of wood and some track with power to it. Your chosen scale determines how long your plank needs to be, as you want to be able to get a decent length of train on to the plank. Now measure your plank, though bear in mind that a nice round figure like 100in or 2m will make things easier, so cut to length accordingly. If your plank is 100in long, prop it up at one end by 1in. You now have a one in one hundred (or 1 per cent) gradient. Try all your locomotives with your heaviest train and they should be able comfortably to haul it up the gradient. Keep adding an inch to the height and repeating until your locomotives start to struggle. You now have an idea of the steepest gradient that your trains can cope with.

Then ease back a bit. You want the gradients to be comfortable for the locomotives, plus you need to future-proof against any new locomotives that may not be as powerful and therefore not able to manage the gradient. Alternatively, you may want to make

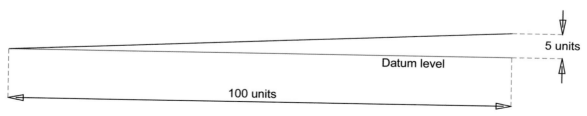

This simple example of a gradient shows that it is necessary to go one hundred units in order to rise five units. This is a 5 per cent gradient, which is also expressed as one in twenty.

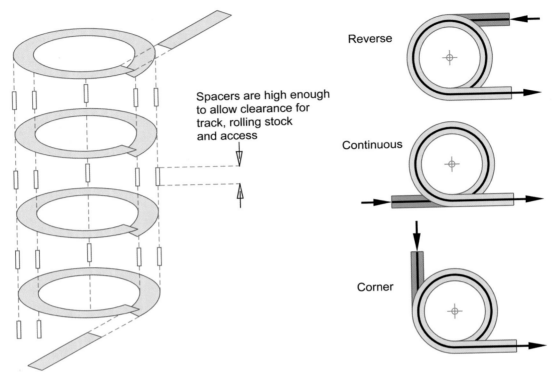

Spacers are high enough to allow clearance for track, rolling stock and access

Reverse

Continuous

Corner

A helix is constructed by joining a series of circular layers that are cut through, so that the end of one layer connects to the beginning of the next. The layers are separated and supported by spacers all the way around the inner and outer edges. Adjusting the entry and exit points creates either a reverse, continuous or corner helix.

your trains longer – just adding one coach could make all the difference. While the trend is towards heavier and therefore more powerful model locomotives, it does no harm to err on the side of caution.

You do not have to have gradients that are only straight lines; as we shall see, trains can climb curves as well. However, do bear in mind that all curves increase the resistance that a train places on the locomotive and its rolling stock, whether on the flat or on a gradient, so you need to take this into account. Once again, err on the side of caution.

With all your empirical data to hand, you will have a figure for the working maximum gradient on your layout. It is now a case of deciding how high you have to go, be it the relatively modest rises of a multi-layer layout, or the considerable rises of a multilevel layout. The resulting answer will probably determine which one of the following methods you use.

THE HELIX

The most impressive of all the solutions is the helix, literally a strip of baseboard that curls around to form a helix linking the lower baseboard to the upper. The advantage of a helix is that the trains just drive off one level on to the other without any need for handling or intervention at all. The helix ensures that both the upper and lower levels remain just that – level. Against this are some pretty serious disadvantages. A helix will take up a lot of space. The relevance of radii to design is very important in terms of how much area a quarter- or half-circle requires. A helix needs a full circle as a base, so whatever your minimum radius is, that defines the footprint required for the helix. While kits for a helix can be purchased, they are pretty tricky things to build unless you are good at a combination of wood-work and engineering. Trains naturally slow down on curves, due to greater resistance, and when going up gradients, and for most of the journey through the helix, the whole train will be on a rising curve. Finally, the length of track curled into a helix can be quite long, so it can take a while for a train to leave one level and arrive at another, the more so the greater the distance between the levels.

A helix can be double-, even triple-tracked, although this is a further engineering complication. However, given the lengthy transfer times, this allows trains at least to move in both directions without a down train having to wait for an up train, as would happen with a single track.

THE LONG GRADIENT

The next method is perhaps a variation on the helix. Instead of curling that long piece of track into a helix, why not unfurl it into a straight line to get from one level to another? By running a track all the way around the outside of your layout, you can get from one level to another. However, you still need quite a bit of distance to go up even a modest height. The sort of small room-sized layouts discussed in this book probably do not offer the required length to get up to the higher level of a multilevel layout, although they are fine for multilayer layouts. There is probably enough of a run for the 'fiddle yard under

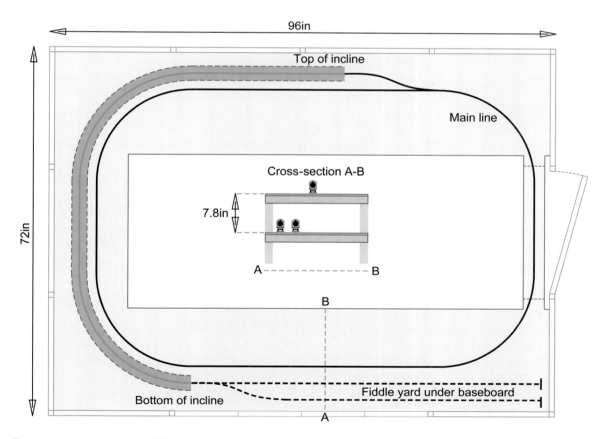

This example assumes an OO gauge layout in a 6ft × 8ft shed (all the measurements are in inches for simplicity). There is a basic main-line loop with 18in radius curves. The incline branches off the outside of the loop and the inclined track is shown in green, a length of 157in. Working to a 5 per cent gradient, the track can drop 7.8in in that distance – more than enough for the height of OO gauge rolling stock and to allow access to the fiddle yard under the baseboard. Alternatively, it could be an incline rising to a terminus over the main line.

the baseboard' approach. Some of the disadvantages of the helix will apply equally to this approach – gradients are still an issue, and you will likely have some curves as well if you have to go all round the room to get the required length.

Consider another approach, again from American practice, of a scenically complete gradient that climbs more or less consistently as it winds around the room. It is another unfurled helix, but with stations along the line. It is, in fact, a complete main line. This is fine if you are just running trains, but it is not going to work if you want sidings and goods yards at the stations unless you face all your sidings downhill or adjust the scenery so that the sidings are on the level, even if the main line is not. The latter option is more complex to build, but the scenic vision, when complete, would be very impressive. After all, real railways are rarely totally on the level, even within the same goods yard.

THE TRAIN LIFT

Like the baseboards, you can make a fiddle yard act in three dimensions by building a train lift. This will allow you to move your trains quite a height in a very short space of time. A train lift is not as complex as it sounds, being a length of baseboard that slides up the wall from one level to the next. By adding a counter weight, it is easy to move up and down. Once again, it requires a modicum of woodwork and engineering skills, but is not too challenging. Think of it as a drawer turned through 90 degrees and attached to a wall instead of a cabinet. Indeed, you can even use a set of long drawer runners to ensure smooth and accurate movement of the train lift.

A lot depends on where you place the train lift. If it is at the end of a baseboard, or in a corner, you can run a train into it, but you will have to reverse it out at the other level. Alternatively, you can swap the locomotive from one end to the other when the train is in the train lift (as you would in a fiddle yard). If you can position the train lift in the middle of the layout, the train can run in one side, switch levels and run out the other side. Make sure that security features are included to cut the power supply to the tracks when the train lift is not on that level, so as to

avoid trains plunging down the lift shaft. As the train lift is long but slim, it could sit at the rear of a scenic section of the layout along one wall.

CASSETTES

The final solution is a much simpler version of the train lift, and it is our old friend the ever versatile system of cassettes. Rather than going to all the trouble and potential complexity of building a train lift, why not just lift a cassette with the whole train from one level to another? If the best place for this changeover point is at the end of a baseboard or in a corner, unlike the train lift, the train can run into the cassette, then you turn the whole cassette around so that the train runs out in the correct direction on the other level.

There are practical limits to using cassettes. Depending on your chosen scale, they can start to get a bit long and unwieldy for longer trains, unless you have equally long arms. A locomotive and four carriages are probably about the maximum for OO gauge. The longer the casettes are, the heavier they will be, depending on how they are made. Using the aluminium angle design will keep things light and strong. Yet even the rolling stock itself can be heavy, especially with the trend of making modern locomotive models heavier to aid traction, with the result that your long cassette may be unbalanced. Make sure you provide 'gates' at the ends of the cassettes before you move them, so as to avoid a train falling out.

UNCONNECTED LEVELS OF THE SAME LAYOUT

If all of these devices to move between levels seem like just too much, ask yourself whether the levels really need to be connected. A lack of connection suggests two totally independent layouts. If the trains passing between the two levels are minimal, consider two versions of the same train, one per level. As a train enters the fiddle yard on the lower level, its doppelgänger can leave the fiddle yard on the upper level to continue the journey. By using some kind of electronic control circuits, this could be achieved automatically. This idea perhaps works best on an

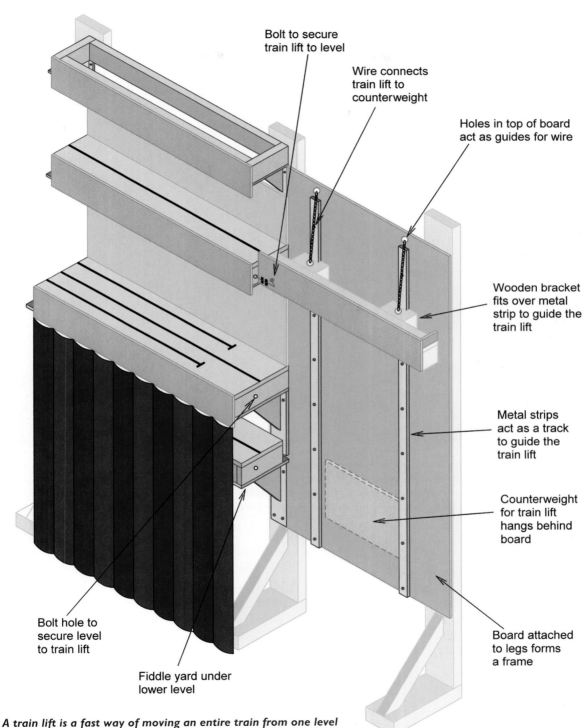

Bolt to secure
train lift to level

Wire connects
train lift to
counterweight

Holes in top of board
act as guides for wire

Wooden bracket
fits over metal
strip to guide the
train lift

Metal strips
act as a track
to guide the
train lift

Counterweight
for train lift
hangs behind
board

Board attached
to legs forms
a frame

Bolt hole to
secure level
to train lift

Fiddle yard under
lower level

*A train lift is a fast way of moving an entire train from one level
to another. This example is at the end of a baseboard, so trains
that run in will have to reverse out. If the baseboards continued to the
right, then as a train exits the train lift on a different level, it can continue in the same direction. Because it is
so quick to move between levels, there is a fiddle yard board behind the curtain and under the lower level.*

Alex Crawford is currently building a multilevel N gauge layout around the walls of a garden shed. Although the two levels are actually unconnected, this photo of one corner shows what a multilevel layout looks like with one level over another. Note also that on the lower level, there are different layers as the tracks at the rear are higher than those in the foreground. (Photo by Alex Crawford)

industrial or yard layout where shunting is mostly self-contained in the respective levels. Otherwise, extensive duplication of stock may be required.

Some of these solutions may seem a little eccentric; however, if you do have a full room at your disposal, the multilevel layout offers a means of doubling that space. All of these ideas, from cassettes to train lifts, have actually been used by railway modellers, so while they may not appeal to you or be wholly appropriate, do take inspiration from them. Wherever there's a will, there is a way, which means wherever there's even a tiny amount of space, there is a way to build yourself a model railway that uses that space to its fullest potential.

CHAPTER SIX

PLANNING YOUR LAYOUT

Planning in this instance is less about the steps to achieve the end result (a project plan) and more about practical design. It does not matter whether you are a computer whiz or more comfortable with pen and paper and a slide rule, as the end result is the same. What you are trying to achieve is a plan that allows you to visualize the finished product before you cut a single piece of timber or lay any track. Being able to see what the layout will look like means that mistakes can be avoided when you come to build it – for example, putting a turnout over a baseboard joint. It provides a firm foundation that will make the

build phase a breeze rather than a chore. Most of all, it gives you a feel for what the model railway layout will look like – if you get excited about the finished plan, just think how much you will enjoy the layout when it is finished.

THE IMPORTANCE OF PLANNING

Planning your model railway can be fun. It might sound like a laborious task, especially when you are impatient to get on with the real fun of actually

Planning is important as it links all the phases of layout construction to avoid mistakes. This view under a layout illustrates the link between track planning and baseboard design. The turnout motor on the right has plenty of space around it, making it easy to install and solder on the wires. The one on the left is right up against the baseboard frame; it even required a bit shaving off the turnout motor to get it to fit.

making the layout. However, try to be patient, take a step back and plan what you are going to do and how you are going to do it. Fools rush in, and it is simply a fact that while you are no fool, if you rush into the construction phase without adequate planning and checking, there is a risk of making a serious mistake that will require a lot of rework to put right. As a rule of thumb, the later a fault in a project is discovered, the more costly it is to put right.

The planning for a model railway does not need reams of architectural diagrams and a flow chart. It is just a case of setting a few hours aside to think about all the things you will need to do, then putting them into a rough yet logical order. Mostly it is common sense and a case of following a logical order, for example you cannot lay track until you have built a baseboard and you cannot do any wiring until the track is laid. Yet you can go wrong. You might lay the track, ballast it and paint the rails, then realize that you need to fit electrical feeds to the rails.

Have I made any mistakes over the years? Of course! On my last layout, I fitted the back scenes before laying the track, which was not a problem until I wanted to spray the track – the rear faces of the rails at the back could not be reached with the aerosol can, so had to be painted by hand. That was a valuable lesson.

Do not be afraid to make mistakes, otherwise you will never get out of your armchair once you finish reading this book. It always helps to plan anything, but it is perhaps all the more important with layouts in a small space. Quite simply, while you can fit in all the elements you want, there is a lot less room for manoeuvre between them and the available space. A lot of the planning is simply a case of that age-old wisdom to 'measure twice and cut once'.

STUDY OTHER PEOPLES' PLANS

When you were at school, you would have been told off for copying someone else's work. As adults, forgery and plagiarism are serious crimes. Fortunately, when it comes to model railways, copying someone else's layout falls into the category of 'imitation is the sincerest form of flattery'. There are many published plans for layouts, either in books of model railway plans, or the numerous magazines that feature other people's layouts.

There is absolutely nothing wrong with slavishly copying someone else's plan. You can, though, inject a little difference. Try mirroring the plan from side to side or from front to back. You may well be forced to make such changes. If a published plan shows the fiddle yard on the right, but your space dictates that your fiddle yard must be on the left, then you have no alternative but to adjust the plan accordingly.

If you have enough room, you may be able to join several plans together from different layouts. Perhaps this could be a through station from one plan combined with the terminus station from another. With a multilevel layout you may find it possible to join two completely separate layout designs in the same space by using a helix or train lift.

It is probably unlikely that you will find a track plan that exactly fits your requirements and in any case you will probably find it hard to resist the temptation to tinker. You may feel that the platforms are not long enough for the trains you want, perhaps the goods yard is too big or too small, and maybe you want to add a small locomotive servicing depot. The point is that published track plans are a huge source of ideas and inspiration. By studying other people's layouts, you will absorb many different ways of doing the same thing. Give these ideas a little time to filter through your imagination and before long you will be inspired to design your own track plan. There may be elements of everyone else's, but the final product will be uniquely your own.

DESIGN THE TRACK PLAN, THEN THE BASEBOARDS

In model railways, which comes first, the track plan or the baseboard? On the one hand, you may design a track plan that gives you everything that you want, then build the baseboards to support it. Alternatively, you may build the baseboards first, then design a track plan to fit them. Which is the right way to do it? The answer is 'a bit of both'.

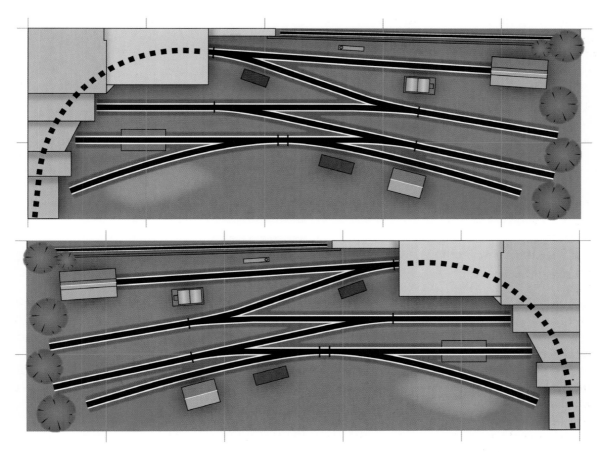

This is a plan of the OO gauge layout 'Denshaw Quarry', expertly drawn by Paul Atkinson. The version at the top represents the layout as it has been built; the one at the bottom is simply a mirror image. Mirroring someone else's plan is a good starting point for developing your own design.

The first task is to measure the available space as if you were going to build the baseboards. For permanent layouts occupying a spare room, garden shed or bookcase, the extremities of the space define what is available for baseboards. Portable layouts such as for a tabletop are a bit more flexible; however, there will still be a limit to the size of the baseboards in terms of what will fit, plus the space available to store the baseboards when not in use. Determine what size baseboards could fit in to the space, but do not build them yet. Now you can design your track plan.

If you design a track plan before you know the maximum size of your baseboards, the chances are you will design a layout that won't fit your available space. When you lay the track, clearances may be tighter than they should be, which can cause problems. Equally, if you build your baseboards before your track plan, the baseboard may start to dictate the track plan. This can occur because of the way baseboards are made. A modest 4ft (1.2m) board will probably be braced across the width every 12in (0.3m). Without taking these cross-braces into consideration, you can bet that at just the place where your track plan says you need to cut a hole in the baseboard to accommodate the turnout motor under the turnout, there will be a piece of timber in the way. I can speak with experience on this matter.

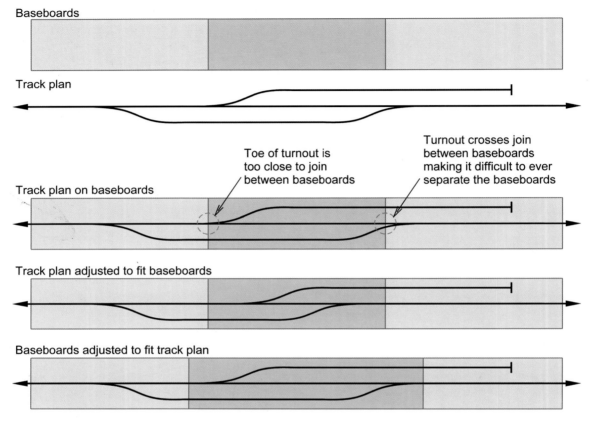

As baseboards can usually be any size, it is better to adjust them to fit the desired track plan, rather than vice-versa.

The track plan may then have to be compromised by moving the turnout one way or another, with the result that a siding or run-round loop becomes longer or shorter than it needs to be, or a combination of both.

If you have done your track plan first, when you come to build the baseboard you will have the prior knowledge of where to put the cross-bracing so that it will not interfere with the turnouts. Turnouts or complicated track can also be avoided where one board joins to another, where the width of the cross-bracing will effectively be double (one for each end of the joining baseboards). Not all baseboards have to be the same length, unless they are to be bolted together facing each other in pairs for storage. This means that the track plan can be split into sections of appropriate baseboard size without

having to compromise the track plan itself. So the order of play is to:

- measure the space available
- determine the maximum length and width of the baseboard surface that will fit the measurements
- design the track plan to fit the maximum measurements
- determine the baseboard sizes that will not interfere with the track plan
- plan where cross-braces will go without interfering with turnouts or compromising the strength of the baseboard.

This advice is valuable whatever scale you are modelling in and no matter how much space you have.

With more generous space, you simply have a bigger margin for error. With a layout in a small space, there is little, if any, room for adjustment, so it pays to get it right first time. It is far easier to rectify a mistake with pen and paper than it is with wood and saw.

DRAWING THE TRACK PLAN

Having done your homework, it is now time to start putting pen to paper and planning your layout. The homework side of things is identifying the parameters that you will be working in – the size of the space, train lengths and minimum radii. With a list of minima and maxima, you will avoid costly mistakes during construction.

This really is the fun part of designing a layout. The ideas you have had, influences such as exhibition layouts seen and classic designs all come together. If you are not sure where to begin, take someone else's plan and modify it to your own particular requirements. Indeed, it is a useful test to try replicating a simple plan while you get the hang of your new planning skills. Be warned though – the planning stage is absorbing and entertaining in its own right and, if you are not careful, you may end up with ten different plans, or never even progress beyond the pen and paper stage.

For the initial 'back of an envelope' designs, do not worry too much about geometry and train lengths, despite what has been said above about the importance of identifying these variables. Simple sketches on a plain piece of paper will help in formulating your track plan preferences. Do you want the platform on the left or the right? Do you want a bay platform? Will the goods shed go on the first siding or the second siding? How about a kickback siding to a small factory? There is no need to work out to the millimetre how long a siding should be if you then decide that you don't want it at the front, you'd rather have it at the back. You can sketch these variations on a theme without recourse to any kind of artistic or draughtsmanship skills at all. When you have a sketch of a track plan that really excites you, it is time to move to the next level of planning.

A track plan may excite you, and you can't wait to build it, but what will it be like to operate? Will you actually get bored very quickly with its operation? Do you know if your layout will work before you build it and how do you go about finding out? This is less of an issue with the room-sized oval layouts, as these are more about watching the trains go by. You can always change the trains, even the whole era, if you get a little bored with the trains that you have. A terminus layout is more focused on operating and shunting. The smaller the layout, the less track, and potentially the less variations of operation. Wouldn't it be great if you could operate the layout before you built it to be doubly sure that it is what you want?

You can draw out the proposed layout a little more formally than a simple sketch and create cardboard templates for the trains, even the wagons, that you will use. If you are still excited about the design while shuffling bits of cardboard around, just think how much you will enjoy operating the completed layout. This simplistic 'operation' of the plan can flush out potential operating problems. Perhaps the dual function of a siding (goods shed and coal merchants) is just too awkward when it is combined with a kickback siding to a factory. Just a few minutes with a pen and another sheet of paper, and you can try a different design that may work better.

By operating this initial design, you get a feel for where things like signals will need to go. If an automated uncoupling system is used, you will need to decide where to put the magnets or solenoids to uncouple the rolling stock. Some of these positions are obvious, such as at the start of a siding, or the extremities of a run-round loop; however, there may just turn out to be another vital place to locate an uncoupler that will make all the difference to the operation. It would be a lot harder to add that extra uncoupler after the track has been laid and the layout is complete.

Now that you have the plan you want and know it is going to be enjoyable to operate, it is time to draw things a little more formally. This is important in order to make sure that it will fit the space you have, that sidings and run-round loops are long

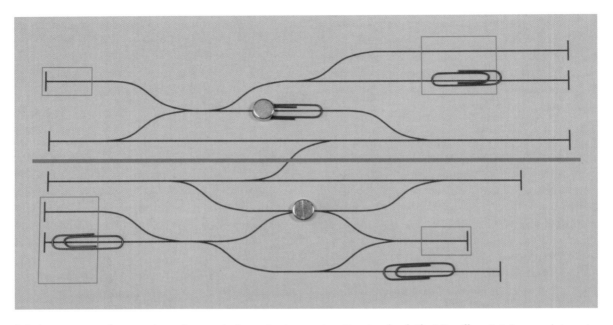

It is important to 'operate' any layout design prior to construction to check that it will maintain your interest. This is a simple drawing of the colliery to gasworks design. Red paperclips represent a rake of coal wagons, blue paperclips are other wagons. Low-powered round magnets are used to represent the locomotive and they 'couple' to one end of a paperclip. Moving the paperclips and magnets around the 'track' gives a very visible demonstration of how the layout will operate.

enough for your rolling stock and trains, and that clearances will be adequate. Having worked out the length of your longest train for the run-round loop, you need to add a little extra to the run-round loop itself so that there is room for the locomotive to safely run past its train without fouling the rolling stock on the other line. If you have a modest plan in a big space, you have plenty of room for error. The smaller the space you are working in, the more important it becomes to check these things. Once you have built a layout, you can't really saw an inch out of the middle of a carriage if the train is too long.

It is not as difficult as it sounds to draw a track plan to scale. Most manufacturers publish the vital statistics of their track components, in particular the turnouts. These dimensions can be halved or quartered to achieve a simple scale drawing. Things can be made easier by using graph paper, adapting the half or quarter scale to the squares on the paper. Curves can be a little tricky. A compass can be used for an exact radius, or, if it is a long, sweeping siding, it can be drawn freehand, as long as you measure where the buffer stop will be in relation to another fixed point. Equally, with turnouts, you know how long a turnout will be, as well as the distance between the tracks, so the curves can be drawn in relation to that. You may even find that the bottom of a tin of beans is just the right curvature for what you need.

The layout need only be drawn to a reduced scale if the actual layout is going to be fairly big, say a room-sized layout. Any layout that is portable (such as a tabletop or bookcase layout, and certainly a micro-layout) can simply be drawn actual size. Even with a room-sized layout that will be in a spare room or a garden shed, it is still perfectly feasible to draw it to actual size. If you think that an A4 pad of paper is not going to be big enough, you would be right; however, there is a cheap and plentiful source of much bigger paper – wallpaper.

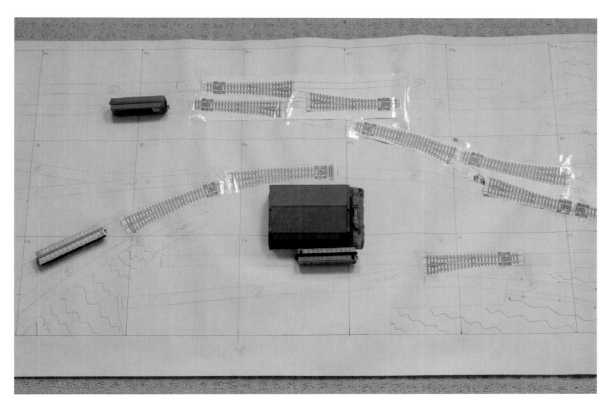

This is a section of a 'wallpaper layout' for N gauge. Each square is 6in (0.15m), so it can be seen that the paper is just over 18in (0.45m) wide. The track plan has been drawn on and turnouts are a mixture of drawn and Peco paper templates. Being actual size, it is possible to place actual buildings and rolling stock on to the plan to check clearances or simply to see how they look.

Most rolls of wall paper are at least 1.5ft (0.45m) wide, so two lengths side by side will cover most likely baseboard depths. Obviously, baseboard length is not an issue for a roll of wallpaper. Check out the end-of-line bin in your DIY store for cheap rolls – as you will be drawing on the back, the pattern on the front is immaterial, although clearly any wallpaper rolls with embossed patterns must be avoided. Best of all is to pay a little more for a roll of lining paper – this is available in very long rolls and in several grades of thickness, the thickest ones being best for standing up to whatever rough handling may be required while you draw and then store the plan. Several years ago I coined the phrase 'wallpaper layouts', these being minimum-space layouts that could be drawn full size on the back of a single piece of wallpaper.

There are several advantages to this approach of drawing out the plan to actual size. First, you will get to really see what the finished layout will look like, albeit in two dimensions. In terms of where buildings will go, you can even see the design in three dimensions by adding a few simple cardboard cut-outs of mock-ups of the buildings. Platforms can be represented by a length of wood. Use a few paperback books with some cardboard on top to show where a bridge will go. You can photograph this three-dimensional creation from different angles to get a feel for how it will look.

The second advantage to a full-scale plan is that rather than 'operating' a scale plan with cardboard cut-out rolling stock, you can put full-size rolling stock on to it. This allows you to see if it looks right,

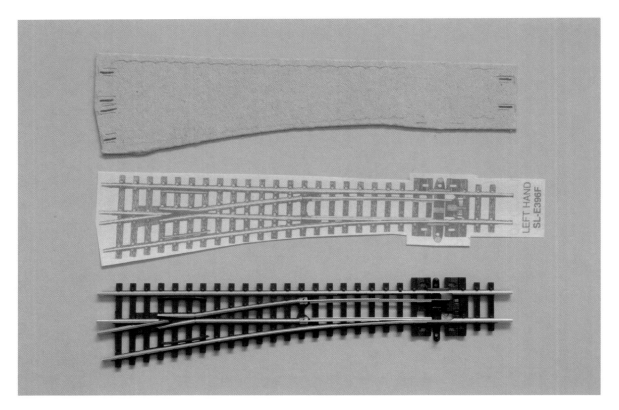

Here are three different ways of representing a Peco Code 55 N gauge turnout when drawing a plan to actual size. At the bottom is the turnout itself; this can be used as a template. In the middle is a paper template for this turnout available from Peco. At the top is a cardboard template made from the actual turnout – note that the rails have been marked in red.

plus it is easier for checking clearances since, rather than trying to work it out, you can see with your own eyes whether or not the loco will fit past the carriages on the run-round loop.

It is probably easier to draw a track plan to full size than to scale because you can use full-size templates. The chances are that you will need to buy at least one, say, left-hand turnout, which you can then draw round to create a simple cardboard template. With proprietary trackwork systems, the right-hand turnout will be an exact mirror image of the left-hand, so all you have to do is turn the template over. An alternative is to use a photocopier to copy the top and bottom of a turnout to create left-hand and right-hand templates; as these are on paper, they can be copied as many times as you want. Similarly,

you can use a computer scanner to get a scale image of the top of a turnout, and then use photo-imaging software to create a mirror image of the turnout. If you are going to use Peco track, all this work is done for you, as the company has an extensive turnout range in all scales, already available as templates that you can photocopy as much as you need. Printed templates are best, as you can see the turnout detail, glue it to the paper plan and see where the ends of the rails are, which makes it easier to line up with the plain track.

For the plain track between the turnouts, you can buy a few pieces of straight and curved track, or a piece of flexi-track. It is then a simple case of running a pencil up both sides of the sleepers to leave an impression of where the track will go.

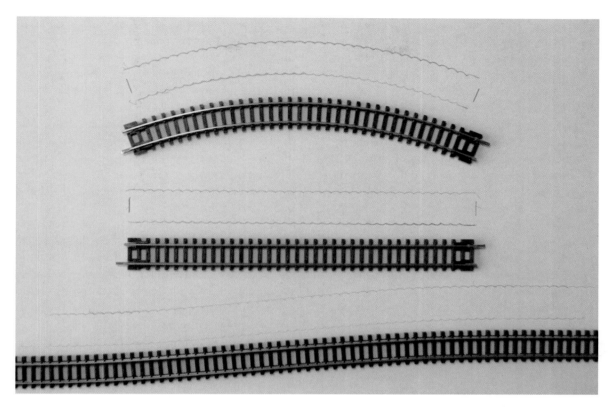

For drawing plain track to full size, just a few pieces of track are needed to use as templates. This is some Peco N gauge track, a 'set track' curve and straight, plus some flexible track at the bottom that can be curved to any shape. If any of the pencil lines are too light, they can be inked in once the plan has been finalized.

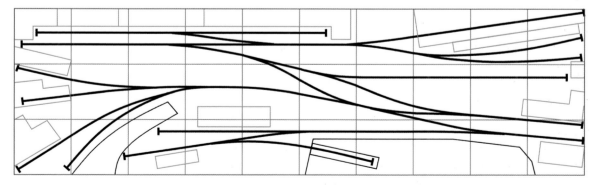

This is the N gauge layout that was drawn to full size on wallpaper now drawn using a simple CAD program. The grid of 6in (0.15m) squares drawn on the wallpaper is replicated on the plan – they act like the grid on a map, making it easier to transfer the detail. This CAD drawing can be printed actual size on about twenty sheets of A4; it is not too onerous a task to join them together to create a full-size plan.

There are some modern hi-tech alternatives using computers, such as modestly priced CAD (Computer Aided Design) programs that are usually quite easy to master. You can draw everything to full size, right down to the millimetre. Such programs allow you to print the design full size, although for larger layouts, you will be stitching together an awful lot of pieces of A4 paper (unless you have a friendly architect with a large plotter type of printer). You can, however, print the drawing at a reduced scale, which is handy if you want to use the cardboard rolling stock templates to assess operation (these templates can be drawn in the CAD program as well). Another advantage to a CAD program is that the final track design can be laid over the baseboard design to ensure that turnouts do not conflict with cross-members.

The best of the track design options using a computer is a bespoke track design program (such as AnyRail). There are now some well-established and very flexible programs, often with proprietary track system components already included. Like the CAD programs, you can print the design full size or scaled down. You are not limited to proprietary turnout sizes, as you can design your own. If you are comfortable building turnouts yourself, you can design and print off a design template for the turnout on which to actually build it (a good example is Templot).

CREATING A MOCK-UP

Whether you use good old-fashioned pen and paper or an up to the minute computer program to design your layout, the plan is only ever going to be two-dimensional. You can get some very sophisticated three-dimensional CAD programs; even a few of the layout design programs will give you a three-dimensional image but none of them can print in three-dimensions. While a two-dimensional plan is fine for a track plan, baseboards, placing buildings and so on, you may find it hard to get a feel for how your layout will actually look.

Visualizing the finished layout is less of a problem in a room-sized layout where the railway line winds through open scenery that is fairly well spaced out. However, it becomes an issue as the design becomes smaller. On a more cramped layout, particularly an urban scene with lots of buildings, it is important to check that all those buildings will not appear to get in each other's way. If you have buildings towards the front of the layout, will they act as effective view blockers as the trains move between scenes, or will they simply obscure the view of the train? Will structures get in the way of accessing the trains where you need to uncouple to perform shunting? Will the layout 'look right'?

To answer these questions, consider building a mock-up of your proposed layout. For small layouts, or micro-layouts, the mock-up can easily be constructed to full scale. You can use anything to roughly sketch out the shape of buildings on the layout. So much comes in packaging these days that it is easy to find boxes of different sizes that will fit the bill. These boxes, particularly the ubiquitous breakfast cereal boxes, provide a ready supply of cheap cardboard that can be chopped up to represent anything from trees to engine sheds. A length of wood can be used to represent a platform.

For slightly larger layouts, you can make a scale model of your scale model. These can be made half or quarter of the size of the final layout design. They are a sort of 'concept model', but they can be useful in visualizing how the completed layout will look, especially if there are lots of buildings and several layers to the layout. Despite using the inside grey-coloured card from packaging, you can end up with a lot of breakfast cereal box packaging, which by its self-promotional nature can be a little garish. Therefore, a quick coat from a cheap aerosol paint spray will give a uniform appearance of the likes of professional architectural models. The uniformity stops the eye being distracted by a mishmash of colours, allowing you to concentrate on how the layout will look.

If the design does not work for you, you can alter the mock-up, or even just chuck it the bin. You will have wasted a lot less time and effort on a mock-up that does not satisfy than building the whole layout and being disappointed. If the design does work, you

A three-dimensional mock-up to actual size brings a two-dimensional plan to life. This simple example in OO gauge uses paperbacks and plastic rulers for a bridge to form a scenic break into the fiddle yard, a scrap of wood for a platform and a roughly torn and folded cereal packet for the station building. A piece of wallpaper represents the baseboard with a grid of 6in (0.15m) squares for reference. While it is not necessary to draw on the actual track plan, the use here of Peco turnout templates gives a feel for where the track will be.

have a three-dimensional 'picture' to refer to while building the actual model railway layout.

TRANSLATING THE PLAN INTO A SHOPPING LIST

Another reason for planning your layout rather than building it in a haphazard manner is that at the end of the planning phase, you can create a shopping list of everything that you need. You will know how many turnouts (and how many of each type) you need, how many yards (metres) of flexible track (or individual track if you are using set track), even how many buffer stops. You will know what buildings you

require and you can look to see if they are available ready to plant, as kits, or whether you will have to scratch-build them. The whole planning and listing purpose prevents you from buying items that do not get used in the end result.

Armed with your shopping list, you can go shopping. Sadly, these days not everywhere has a local model shop, so the chances are that you will have to make a special trip, or order by post. It is helpful, therefore, to know in advance everything that you will need. It is extremely frustrating to make a start on your layout, then realize you have forgotten a vital component.

CHAPTER SEVEN

BASEBOARDS

All model railway layouts need a baseboard no matter how big or small they are. They are literally the foundation on which you will build. There are many books and much wisdom about how to build baseboards. There are, however, several aspects that bear particular study in relation to model railway layouts in a small space. These are mainly in relation to portability – many of the suggestions in this book create space by temporarily occupying someone else's space. Therefore, an easily portable solution is essential, the main requirement for portable baseboards being that they should be robust yet lightweight. Similarly, where a whole room is available for a permanent solution, do not restrict your imagination by thinking that a doorway is an obstacle – there are lightweight solutions that will bridge the gap.

EVEN PERMANENT LAYOUTS SHOULD BE PORTABLE

The potential spaces for layouts outlined in this book mean that layouts will either be permanent or portable. If you only have a temporary space on which to use your layout, such as a tabletop, obviously your layout will need to be portable. If you have a permanent space, such as a spare room, you can have a permanent layout. However, even permanent layouts should be portable.

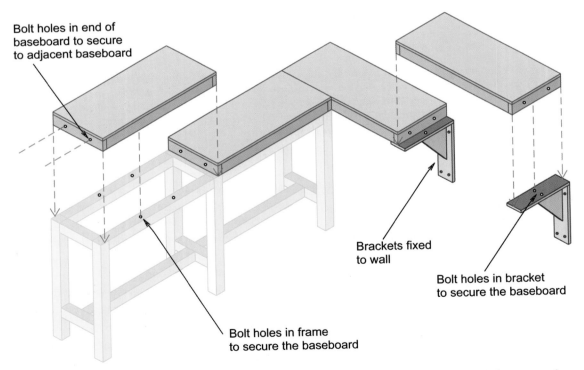

Bolt holes in end of baseboard to secure to adjacent baseboard

Brackets fixed to wall

Bolt holes in bracket to secure the baseboard

Bolt holes in frame to secure the baseboard

By building the baseboards so that they bolt to each other and to their supports, the whole layout can be disassembled if required. It also makes it easier to work on individual baseboards during construction; they can be removed and worked on in a different place, or turned over when fitting the wiring underneath. The baseboards can be supported on brackets screwed to walls or on freestanding frames.

The reason for this contradictory statement is that you never know what's round the corner. Imagine just getting your layout finished in a garden shed, only to find that the garden needs to be dug up right through your shed to fix the drains. For modellers, this can be as disruptive as a complete house move.

There is a temptation literally to screw your layout to every piece of floor and wall for a simple construction and for strength. Strong it will be, but it will be impossible to remove the layout without the risk of some serious damage to it. Even if you fix the supports to the layout, such as to store a bed under it, or if it is a shelf layout, make sure that the baseboards themselves are simply bolted on and thus easy to remove – you can always build new supports in the new home if the layout is going far.

By designing portability into a layout from the beginning, you will actually find it easier to build. For example, you might want to take it outside to spray-paint the track, which you can do with individual baseboards. The biggest advantage will be when you come to do the layout wiring, as you can put each baseboard on its side for easy access underneath. Otherwise, you are left with the challenge of crawl-ing around underneath the baseboard while waving a hot soldering iron – more than a little uncomfortable and a tad dangerous.

WEIGHT

As we get older, everything seems to get heavier. There are plenty of modellers who will swear that the baseboards of their portable layouts have got heavier over the years. You cannot change the laws of physics, but you can change the way that you design and build your baseboards. Almost without exception, baseboards are made of wood. In America, a lot of modellers make use of the thick foam sheets that are used in building construction. A few adventurous modellers have used foam board (the stuff used for life-size cut-outs in the cinema and retail displays), but it is safe to say that wood is the material of choice for 99 per cent of base-boards.

Weight is of vital importance if your layout will be moved on a regular basis. I once lived in a house where a small layout was stored in a cupboard above a wardrobe in the upstairs bedroom; it was actually operated in the back room downstairs. There was a lot of lifting and carrying involved from storage to the place of use. Imagine having to lift a layout above head height to get it into a storage cupboard. This experience served to emphasize the importance of the weight of a layout.

Not all wood is the same. It comes in varying types and qualities. Some are to be avoided at all costs, such as chipboard, which is extremely heavy and hard to cut. Great consideration needs to be given to what the frame and the top of the baseboard will be made out of.

A TRADITIONAL 'TWO BY ONE INCH' FRAME

The traditional baseboard frame has been made for many years out of 2in by 1in (50mm by 25mm) timber. It is easy to cut and then glue and screw together to make a frame, with cross-members to support the top. It is perfectly adequate for a baseboard of about 4ft (1.2m) long by 2ft (0.6m) wide. To make the baseboard larger, it may be better to use the next size up of timber. If you are using equipment under the baseboard, such as slow-acting turnout motors, you will need a much deeper baseboard frame to accommodate these larger objects. However, bigger pieces of wood will make the baseboard heavier. For modest-sized boards on simple portable layouts, the 'two by one inch' framed baseboard is still as viable today as it ever was.

THE PLYWOOD BEAM

There is, however, a popular alternative, which is the plywood beam. This is a sandwich of two sheets of plywood, with softwood blocks in-between to act as spacers. The use of plywood and a lot of fresh air between the spacers makes the beams much lighter. The beams need to be deeper than a tradi-tional 'two by one inch' frame, at least 3in (75mm) in order to have strength, which is handy if you have a lot of big turnout motors and mechanisms

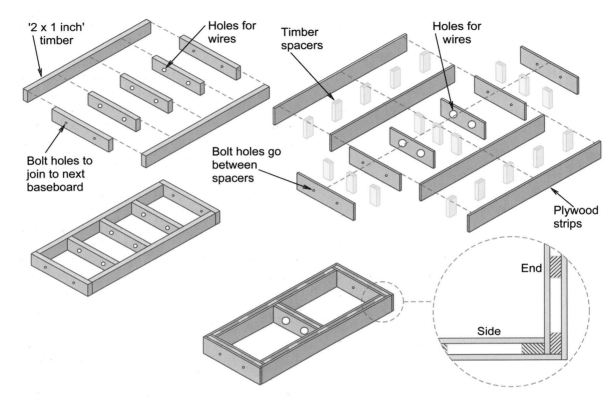

The traditional baseboard frame (seen on the left) is simple to construct from 'two by one inch' timber. The plywood beam frame (seen on the right) is more complex, with its lamination of plywood strips and softwood spacers; however, it is lighter and actually stronger.

for signals and so on. The plywood beam baseboard appears to be twice as large as a traditional frame, but it will be half the weight. Like the traditional design, the larger the baseboard, the thicker the plywood that will be needed. I have used plywood as thin as ³⁄₁₆in (4mm) on a small portable layout and it is still in one piece.

For any baseboard below 3ft (0.9m) long and 1ft (0.3m) wide, the traditional 'two by one inch' frame is probably best, as the small size of the layout or baseboard means that weight should not be an issue. If you plan to use baseboards larger than that, do give the plywood beam frame serious consideration. If you are worried about accurately cutting strips of plywood from a big sheet, check with your local DIY store or timber merchant, as they will usually cut it for you, often for no extra charge.

BASEBOARD TOPPINGS

Having determined the frame for your baseboard, you need to add a top, unless you are building an open-topped frame for maximum rural scenic potential. A very popular choice is ³⁄₈in (9mm) Sundeala. It is not too heavy, is quite easy to cut and it takes track pins very easily. However, it can be prone to sagging if it is not properly supported by a sufficient number of cross-members.

An increasingly popular choice is MDF (Medium Density Fibreboard), which is available in a range of thicknesses. Generally, ⁵⁄₁₆in (8mm) MDF is quite sufficient for a baseboard top; it is a much harder material than Sundeala, but will still take track pins if you are careful. It is also much heavier. It is a good material for a permanent layout that may see only occasional movement, but for a portable layout, you could be doubling the weight of the baseboard. As with the frame, for a 3ft by 1ft (0.9m by 0.3m) baseboard, as you might have for a micro-layout, it is less of an issue. Anything larger and you could find yourself struggling to move the baseboards easily.

As with the baseboard frame, plywood can come to the rescue. A thin sheet of plywood is perfectly adequate for a baseboard top. Since the plywood beam method makes a strong frame, there is no need to rely on the baseboard top to contribute to the strength of the complete baseboard. If you wanted to be sure, you could use the sandwich principle once again, with two baseboard tops separated by wooden blocks; this would also give you the opportunity to add simple scenic features below track level, such as a bridge over a stream.

One final advantage to lightweight baseboards that are portable even for a permanent layout is that they are easier to work on when you are building the layout. For example, you can easily take the whole baseboard outside if you want to use an aerosol spray to paint the track. Any modeller will tell you that trying to complete the electrical wiring under a baseboard is at best difficult and, at worst, an exercise in extreme yoga. If you can lift the baseboard up to 90 degrees, all your wiring can be done from the comfort of a chair.

There are some very good reasons for keeping your baseboards light but strong. The last thing you want is to build an immovable object, as you will then most likely feel less inclined to get it out to enjoy the operation of your finished layout.

BRIDGING THE GAP

A common feature of sheds, garages and spare bedrooms is that in order to have an oval layout that gives a continuous circuit, the gap created by the doorway will need to be bridged. There are three methods to achieve this: a duck-under; a lift-out section; and a lift-up section.

DUCK-UNDER

A duck-under is perhaps not really a method, since it means having a permanent (or permanently portable)

baseboard to bridge the gap. It is necessary to 'duck under' such an arrangement. Its suitability to your requirements largely depends on how fit and nimble you are at ducking under a baseboard. If the baseboard is set at tabletop height, it is likely that you will have to crawl under the baseboard. If the baseboard is at a higher level and you are of average height, you may be able to limbo under it more easily. However, it is an arrangement that stands to become a nuisance all too quickly.

If you make the baseboard in front of a doorway as deep as the rest of your layout to accommodate scenery or curves, then you are effectively making a tunnel for yourself. Even at an elevated height, you will struggle to 'duck under' without banging your head. To mitigate this problem, you can design the connecting board to be much narrower. Preferably, it should contain just the one or two main-line tracks that are required to make the circuit. As a result, you will probably not add scenery to this baseboard, so the opposite ends will likely need a scenic break, the best candidate being tunnel mouths.

A duck-under is to be expected to be used in a garden shed as the doors usually open outwards. If you build a duck-under in a room where the door opens inwards, then you will potentially lose a considerable corner of space to accommodate the arc of the door.

LIFT-OUT SECTION

A gentler solution on your back and knees is to use a lift-out section. Besides removing the need to crawl into the room, another immediate advantage is that you can place the baseboard right in front of the door. The only drawback is that you have to move the baseboard every time you or someone else wants to enter or exit the room. It could become a bit like a level crossing – you have to wait until the train has passed by before the barrier can be lifted. Bearing ingress and egress in mind, a lift-up section (see below) is probably a better solution.

A lift-out section is easy to build. It is just another baseboard, though not as long, as it only needs to be slightly greater than the width of the doorway. When you build your supporting frame for the

This is the lift-out section on Colin Whalley's OO gauge layout. This first photo shows it in position – the lift-out section is on the left (visible top left is the fact that it is slightly narrower). The track is laid over a sound-insulating underlay; at the gap this has been replaced with a strip of plywood. Copper-coated Paxolin is glued to the plywood instead of sleepers. The rails are soldered to the copper to keep them perfectly aligned. Sections are then cut into the copper coating between each track and each rail for electrical isolation.

baseboards, allow a 'shelf' at each end where the lift-out baseboard will go. The lift-out section simply sits on the 'shelf' at either side. There are several things to consider in the design. Most important is weight. If you are regularly lifting a section in and out, perhaps several times during an operating session, then a heavy baseboard made from thick timbers and a substantial MDF covering will get heavier and heavier each time you move it.

As with the duck-under, consider whether you need a full-depth baseboard for scenery, or whether a thin 'plank' with just the running lines will suffice. If you opt for the thin plank, make sure that you add simple plywood faces just in case a train derails, as you would not want it to tumble to the floor.

If the bare appearance of the lift-out section does not please aesthetically, it can be disguised to look like a bridge. If you want the full-depth baseboard, consider a lightweight construction using plywood beams and a thin plywood top to reduce weight. Such a construction makes a solid, though light-weight, box, the only drawback being that the box can act like a drum as trains pass over. Compensate for this by using a foam covering on the baseboard top to soak up the vibration and noise.

In order to remove the lift-out section completely, it cannot have any permanently attached wires, nor can the rails be joined to the other baseboards to supply electricity. Therefore, simple but effective solutions are required to supply electricity.

This photo shows Colin Whalley's lift-out section actually lifted out and placed on its side. This reveals the ledge on the permanent baseboard on which the lift-out section simply rests. A piece of thin plastic strip has been glued on top of the ledge to get the height absolutely perfect. In the middle front of the ledge can be seen the socket for the plug on the lift-out section. The plug/socket combination may look overly substantial, even for the DCC bus wires carrying a higher current, but such fittings will be more durable over time.

The most obvious and robust one is to use a plug and socket. Such an arrangement is only required at one end; however, you do have to remember to unplug before you lift out. Another solution is to install contacts on the 'shelf' that supports the lift-out baseboard with corresponding contacts under the ends of the lift-out baseboard itself. You can buy copper-coated Paxolin strip and all manner of copper wires to achieve this.

LIFT-UP SECTION

The lift-up section is just a slightly more user-friendly variation of the lift-out section. If you have ever observed the speed with which a barman exits the bar using a lift-up flap, you will recognize the efficiency of the arrangement. In the lift-up section the removable baseboard is hinged at one end, so that it lifts up to 90 degrees. You only need the 'shelf'

arrangement to support the baseboard at the non-hinged end. As the baseboard is not completely removed, the wiring can be permanently attached at the hinged end with sufficient slack to allow for the upwards movement of the baseboard. Some way of safely retaining the baseboard in the vertical position needs to be incorporated unless you are prepared to lift up and then let down every time you pass through. Even a modest-sized lift-up baseboard will give you a nasty bump if it swings down on you.

As the lift-up section will be by the doorway, consider a simple hook and loop arrangement of the type used to hold garden gates in the open position. As with lift-out baseboards, do consider the weight when designing and building, though the hinge will support much of the weight. Constructing a lift-up section does require a little more precision than a simple lift-out section in order to get the clearances

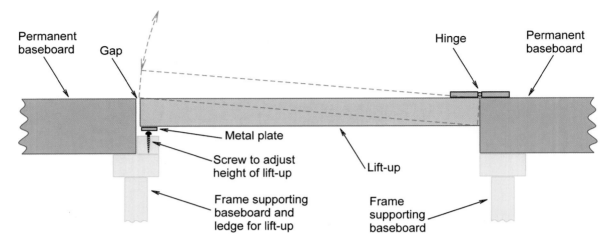

A lift-up section is fairly easy to build and the simplest to use of all the bridging solutions. It is hinged at one end with nothing more sophisticated than a pair of ordinary door hinges. At the other end, a metal plate rests on a number of screws on a ledge – these provide a simple way of levelling the lift-up section with the adjacent baseboard. There also needs to be a gap – big enough to allow the lower edge of the lift-up section to clear the edge of the baseboard, but small enough to stop wheels derailing. As the lift-up will be shorter and narrower than the baseboards, it does not have to be as deep to maintain its strength.

correct where the end of the section meets the adjoining baseboard.

CONSIDERATIONS FOR GAP SOLUTIONS

Where a section of baseboard is an easily removed lift-up or lift-out section, consider incorporating some kind of safety device to avoid trains plummeting into an abyss. Otherwise, you can be sure that one day you will be distracted and forget and your most expensive train will take a nasty tumble. The simplest device is some kind of easily installed guard rail over the end, perhaps slotted into holes in the supporting 'shelf' – the worst that happens is that the train bumps into this and gets a bent buffer or two. However, you have to remember to put the barrier in place. A fool-proof solution is an electrical one. By installing 'push to make' plunger switches under the lift-out section, a circuit can be broken when the baseboard is removed, thereby isolating the sections of track either side of the gap. Remember to allow enough stopping distance for that fast-moving express train.

As rail joiners cannot be used to connect the track where it must be broken for lift-out and lift-up sections, it is worth soldering the ends of the rails to copper-coated Paxolin strips to hold them in gauge. This will prevent derailments at the gap.

The only other cause of derailment may be the wood itself, as wood naturally expands and contracts depending on the dampness of the climate – for example, a lift-out section may have a tendency to stick fast in the summer but be easily removed in the winter. This is more likely to happen in a shed or garage than in a centrally heated spare bedroom. The movement of the wood can make rails higher, which may cause a derailment; therefore, it is worth considering some simple adjustment to raise or lower the ends of the lift-out baseboard. Adding a screw at each corner allows for simple adjustment, although plastic shims can be used to equally good effect. This is one thing in favour of the duck-under, as its permanency means that it is not affected in this way. You can mitigate against movement in the wood used to make the baseboards by buying good-quality wood and sealing the timbers with a good varnish.

CHAPTER EIGHT

CLASSIC DESIGNS

Despite the recreation of railway engineering in miniature, model railways is also a creative hobby, both as an expression of artistic creation and the natural desire to solve the challenges of how actually to create. You can gain a huge amount of inspiration from looking at other people's layouts. Thank goodness that model railways is a hobby where imitation is the sincerest form of flattery. No one will mind if you slavishly follow their layout design. Many a modeller has seen another layout and thought, 'That's just what I want!' Some modellers have even bought a layout when it was offered for sale.

All model railway layouts offer some inspiration, yet some are considered truly timeless. They have been copied and reworked by many modellers over several decades. These are the classic layouts that have been built in one form or another by generations of modellers. You may decide to follow in their footsteps. There's nothing wrong with using someone else's design as a starting point and then adapting it to suit your needs. Some are referred to by modellers by name, such as 'Inglenook Sidings' or 'Minories', while others are generic situations like a motive power depot or a goods yard.

'INGLENOOK SIDINGS'

When I spent time as a volunteer on a preserved railway, one of the roles undertaken was that of a shunter. You might think that the locomotive driver is the one in charge, but, actually, in a goods yard, it is the shunter who gives the orders. The shunter is responsible for moving wagons as efficiently and safely as possible and to do this he will tell the locomotive driver what to do. It is a very challenging role and, sometimes, with a yard full of wagons, a limited headshunt and lots of wagons to move around, it is like trying to solve a complex puzzle. So why not try to capture this intellectual challenge in a model railway?

There was a time when so-called 'shunting-puzzle' layouts were quite popular. The idea was to design a fiendishly difficult track layout, then set the challenge of operating it. It is hugely absorbing fun, yet they seemed to fall out of favour with modellers, being seen as more akin to train sets than 'proper' model railways. Nothing could be further from the truth. Many layouts are operated without timetables and wagons are shunted at whim. The shunting-puzzle layout has a purpose; you can think of an imaginary customer requesting wagons to be delivered to certain sidings, or a train being assembled before being worked up a branch line. These functions give the layout a purpose. The idea of a shunting-puzzle layout is to make something that is very challenging to operate as a shunter. The father of all shunting-puzzle layouts is generically referred to as 'Inglenook Sidings'.

The concept of 'Inglenook Sidings' as a shunting-puzzle layout is believed to have been created by A. R. Walkley as long ago as 1925. A small layout of that name and with the now classic track plan was exhibited by Alan Wright in the late 1970s. It consists of the 'sidings' of the name and a headshunt to feed them. The sidings are deliberately short, the longest capable of holding five wagons and the shortest only three. The headshunt can only accommodate a loco and three wagons. It helps if all the wagons are the same length; using the extensive range of commercially available 10ft wheelbase wagons is a good starting point. There are eight wagons on the layout and the objective of the 'game' is to assemble a train of five wagons in a certain order as dictated by randomly dealt cards. These cards can be as 'low-tech' as playing cards, or as 'hi-tech' as bespoke cards with photographs of the actual wagons taken with a digital camera. It sounds simple, but the limited space requires careful planning to achieve the goal. You can test your mettle by trying to assemble the train with the smallest number of moves possible.

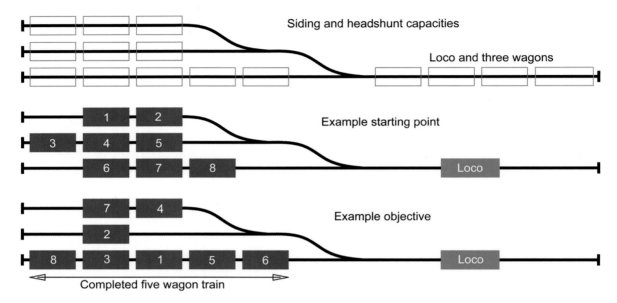

'Inglenook Sidings' is the classic shunting-puzzle layout. The siding and headshunt capacities are shown in the top diagram. The middle diagram shows an example starting point with an example objective shown in the bottom diagram, to get the wagons into the order 8, 3, 1, 5, 6. Try having a go – it is not as easy as it seems. You can adapt this plan to make it more complicated, or incorporate it into a larger layout, yet it shows that even a simple plan can be extremely absorbing.

The modest scope of this layout means that it's a real space saver and it is perfectly possible in a small space using any scale. There is scope for some additional space saving by making the headshunt part of a fiddle yard. This could be a simple one-track extension to the main board that contains the sidings, or you could use cassettes that allow you to change the wagons on the layout. The original 'Inglenook Sidings' concept was for just three sidings, which requires only two turnouts; however, there is nothing to stop you having extra sidings and making the 'game' as simple or as complicated as you want. Many modellers are still playing the shunting puzzle of 'Inglenook Sidings'. You may not immediately recognize the design and the more serious modellers may deny it, but if they are having fun shunting wagons in a confined yard, they are keeping the idea well and truly alive.

'ASHBURTON'

There was a time when modellers bemoaned the appearance of yet another variation of the 'Ashburton' layout. If ever there was a model railway that epitomized the idea that a design can be considered a classic if it is endlessly copied, then this is the one. There is a very good reason why. While Ashburton was a sleepy Great Western Railway terminus, you will see many layouts from steam era to modern era with their roots firmly traced back to this station. It is a design that offers you passenger trains, goods trains, even a locomotive shed, all in a small space – no wonder most of us still love it after all these years.

The key features of the small terminus layout are basically a platform for passenger trains, modest goods facilities and a run-round loop. A simple branch-line passenger service is unlikely to need two platforms; however, you can add another one if you have the space, or consider using a bay platform

This photo shows the full scenic extent of N gauge layout 'Unnycoombe', a classic Great Western Railway terminus in the 'Ashburton' style by Chris Ford and Nigel Hill. Although only using four turnouts, there is a station, run-round loop, cattle dock, bay platform and goods siding occupying just 43in by 12in (1m by 0.3m). (Photo by Steve Flint courtesy of Peco Publications and Publicity Ltd)

on the opposite platform face. A run-round loop is essential, although the Great Western Railway used auto-coach trains that could be driven from the coach or locomotive, thus negating the need for a run-round, just like modern diesel multiple units (DMUs).

If you want to run any goods trains, you will need a run-round loop. Goods facilities need be little more than a single siding, which can have any, or all, of a goods shed, some coal staithes, a loading dock or a cattle dock. If you have the room, try to split these facilities over several sidings, although both approaches are just as challenging to operate for the shunter. As well as auto-coaches and DMUs, goods trains can arrive, shunt the siding and run round (getting the brake van on the other end requires a bit of shunting in itself). You can consider a private siding, perhaps serving a dairy or a factory to add a little extra interest. Such industries require substantial buildings, which can be used to disguise the fiddle yard, thus making the most of your baseboards.

For those who feel that this is still a bit limiting and if you have a bit more space, then change the terminus into a through station – this time, the run-round loop becomes a passing loop, which enables two trains to be in the station at one time. An additional fiddle yard would be required at the other end, but the simplest solution would be an oval configuration to a rear fiddle yard, as this requires minimal stock handling and the option simply to sit back and watch the trains go by.

'MINORIES'

The late Cyril Freezer created the 'Minories' layout concept more than fifty years ago and it is still

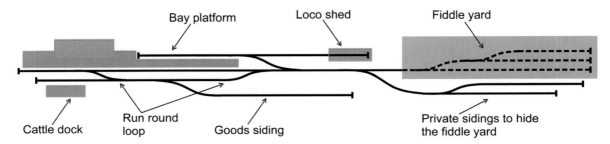

Bay platform   Loco shed   Fiddle yard

Cattle dock   Run round loop   Goods siding   Private sidings to hide the fiddle yard

This plan is only loosely based on 'Ashburton', but it serves to illustrate the elements of a small terminus station. You can include as many of these elements as you wish. The plan is not era-specific; it can easily be updated to the modern era by replacing the cattle dock with an oil terminal and the loco shed with a stabling point.

going strong. This idea takes us from the small rural station of Ashburton to a medium-sized town or city terminus. The long platforms can accommodate three- or four-coach trains with a locomotive, or DMUs and electric multiple units (EMUs). The focus here is on passenger operation, either a busy city commuter station, or a modest town station with regional and local trains. You need a bit of length for this design, but not a lot of width. It can be accommodated on a bookcase or shelf, or even in a small room or garden shed. Remember that you will need a fiddle yard of approximately the same length as the station itself, since it must receive and dispatch trains that are of equal length as the longest platform in the station.

Parcels trains are a logical extension of passenger trains, but there are no real goods facilities. You could build a modest goods yard or motive power depot just before the station itself if you have enough length. The latter will add another layer of operational interest, as the locomotives arriving on passenger trains need to be serviced. If a room or shed is available, the station can be put down one side and the fiddle yard down the other, while the half-circle at the top of the room can accommodate a motive power depot or goods yard. Unlike a room-filling oval layout, this layout does not create problems regarding doorways. However, there is nothing to stop you taking the track past the door and developing the concept into a through station if you want to.

'Ripper Street' is an OO gauge layout by the Thames Valley Area Group of the Diesel and Electric Modellers United (DEMU) society that simply exudes the kind of urban atmosphere of a 'Minories'-type layout. Note how there are three platform faces to service an intensive passenger service. (Photo by Ian Manderson courtesy of Peco Publications and Publicity Ltd)

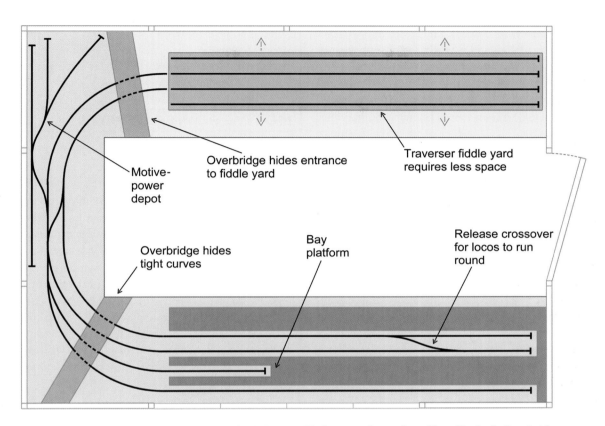

This is an OO gauge 'Minories'-style plan folded into a U-shape to fit inside a 6ft × 8ft shed. Overbridges are used to hide tight 18in (0.46m) radius curves and break the layout into three sections (station, motive power depot and fiddle yard). An interesting variation would be to replace the fiddle yard with another terminus station to allow end-to-end running; the motive power depot between them could be imagined to serve either station, as it is 'isolated' from them by the overbridges.

Many termini have release crossovers at the inner ends of the platform in order to release the locomotive from the incoming train – effectively a run-round loop. You do not need a release crossover, as you can operate the station with a shunt release; a station pilot pulls the coaches out and propels them into an adjacent platform, thereby releasing the 'trapped' train locomotive, which can then back on to the coaches. An alternative is to use a spare locomotive simply to back on to the coaches and, when it departs, the trapped locomotive is released ready to be used on the next train to come in.

By choosing an urban setting, Cyril Freezer cleverly chose a setting that is ideally suited to a long, narrow layout, as befits a station. The background

and back scene can be disguised with buildings, but forced perspective and selective compression can still be used to give a deeper feel to the layout. However, the design assumes deep cuttings and high retaining walls, as would be found in the urban environment, and these alone are perfectly acceptable as a backdrop.

You only need two turnouts to serve three platform faces, which is surely enough for a medium-sized town or city terminus. If you do not use one of the three platforms as, say, a parcels platform, you could use a kickback siding to serve a parcels depot, or perhaps a goods depot, depending on your chosen era. This would allow for a greater variety of stock than just passenger stock, with some parcels vans (which always come in a huge variety, whatever period you model) and maybe a few goods wagons. Alternatively, and especially useful if you are using a spare locomotive to take the train out, you could use the siding as a stabling point, with capacity for several locos, and maybe even a small refuelling point (which requires either coal bunkers or oil tanks depending on your period). Stabling and refuelling could be off-stage, which gives the excuse for light engine movements to and from the station. As a terminus to fiddle yard-type plan, if you take the parcels/goods depot option, the siding could be extended for quite a way so that it runs in front of the fiddle yard. The associated depot (often very large structures in urban environments) could be used to help disguise the fiddle yard.

There is a lot of potential here for a busy operational layout with some decent-sized passenger trains, maybe a bit of freight and plenty of locomotive movements, which is what Cyril Freezer always envisaged. At the time that he first published the design, it was just one of the many ideas for layouts that he had. The name he chose has come to represent a generic type of layout; say 'Minories' to most

railway modellers and they know exactly the type of layout to which you are referring. That surely makes it a classic and well worth looking at once again as inspiration for your layout.

MOTIVE POWER DEPOTS

I have had the chance to walk around real motive power depots, both steam and diesel. In reality, they are big places. Locomotive sheds are cavernous when you are inside them and there seems to be just as much real estate when you go outside. Yet by careful selective compression you can have all the key characteristics of a motive power depot in a small space. This small space can be a portion of a larger layout, such as an oval layout or the 'Minories' type. It may just be the layout itself. If you have a large collection of locomotives, what better way to show them off? For many modellers, it is the locomotives that are the most important thing, especially if they bring back memories of train spotting, perhaps even a bit of 'shed bashing' as well.

The major motive power depots have always been big affairs, but the smaller sub-sheds might have been

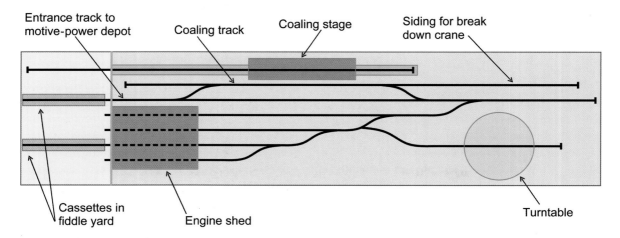

This is a generic plan for a steam-era motive power depot. An entrance track takes locos past the coaling stage for refuelling, then to a kickback that leads to a ladder of four tracks, which enter the engine shed (just the front of which is modelled). These tracks pass through the back scene to cassettes in the fiddle yard (a traverser would be an alternative), allowing more engines to enter the shed than will actually fit. An elevated line at the back supplies coal wagons to the coaling stage. This plan works just as well for the modern era; just replace the coaling stage and turntable with diesel refuelling equipment.

At the other extreme of locomotive servicing facilities is this example on 'Denshaw Quarry' in OO gauge, typical of the limited amenities to be found in an industrial or dockyard setting. An engine shed, some fuel tanks, a few rusty wheels and some welding equipment are all that are needed to make a nice scene on any layout, whether large or small.

much more modest, even just a single track shed at the end of a branch line. The modern equivalent is the stabling point where locomotives wait between duties, with perhaps some basic fuelling capabilities. There are lots of books about motive power depots, locomotive sheds and locomotives themselves, so there is plenty of inspiration to be had (especially as 'shed bashing' is more severely frowned upon now than it ever was).

You do not necessarily have to model all the elements of a motive power depot. The key features are a locomotive shed, fuelling (either coal or diesel), a turntable (for the steam era) and repair facilities (possibly a large crane for lifting a locomotive). Any one of these features on its own tells a railway enthusiast straight away that the scene is a motive power depot. For example, you may just model a coaling stage – they are fascinating buildings with a procession of locomotives passing through and even a few coal wagons to keep them supplied. The rest of the motive power depot facilities can be off-stage. In the same way that a fiddle yard represents the rest of the railway network, it can also represent the remainder of the immediate railway location that you are trying to portray. The entirety of the layout could just be the locomotive shed, especially the roundhouse type with one or more turntables inside (think of the National Railway Museum at York). The fiddle yard could be a series of simple cassettes that each holds a locomotive, entering the shed from different sides. This sort of a compact layout would be ideal for a tabletop.

Motive power depots are busy places, as the railway seeks to minimize down time for its expensive assets. There is plenty of interesting operation to be had as locomotives come in and out, get serviced, repaired and turned if necessary. Do not think that this representation of just a single railway function is limiting in any way. Motive power depots are one of the most challenging scenes to get right – they can be more evocative of a time and place than any other piece of the railway.

GOODS YARDS

Like motive power depots, goods yards are big places, but they also come in all shapes and sizes. Fortunately for those of us working in a smaller space, that's good news. Another plus point is that there is no right or wrong way to design a goods yard. There is no rule or formula that says they must have a certain number of sidings or facilities.

In the rural outposts along sleepy branch lines, the goods yard often consisted of just one siding. Very few of the goods that railways carried required specialist loading and unloading facilities. Most of it could be unloaded by manhandling out of vans and shovelling out of open wagons, with loading just being the reverse. A simple yard crane could handle anything that a couple of blokes could not lift by themselves. In the steam era, labour was cheap and plentiful, so there were always a couple of blokes to hand. Most of the specialized facilities were no more than a loading dock for wheeled goods, or a cattle dock in farming areas. Therefore, even a simple single-siding goods yard could see a lot of comings and goings of a variety of wagons.

OPPOSITE: 'Bonnington Goods' by Bob Rowlands is an OO gauge layout without a station. As the name suggests, it represents just a goods yard and is based on an actual location in Edinburgh away from the main line. Such commercial districts would have been a hive of activity in the steam era, so there's plenty of absorbing action for the operator. (Photo by Steve Flint courtesy of Peco Publications and Publicity Ltd)

These single-line goods yards were not always part of a station. A siding belonging to the railway company would almost certainly be found at the station so that the station master could keep an eye on things. A private siding, however, could be anywhere along the line; it would be situated where the customer was, not where the station was. Like a goods yard, a private siding could be just one track, or a whole series of sidings. The larger concerns would even have their own locomotive for shunting. Therefore, it is not necessary to have a station in order to have a goods yard. In a room-sized layout, or a tabletop layout in the smaller scales, you could have a simple loop supplying trains in either direction through a scene, with the only sidings being to a private concern that could be shunted by the train locomotive or a private shunter.

Some of these private sidings were just a part of a huge factory complex, so big, in fact, that the company would have not one shunting locomotive, but a whole fleet, even its own motive power depot. A factory complex is just another variation of a goods yard, with sheds, loading docks and cranes scattered around the site. These places make great layouts and are huge fun to operate.

Be it a goods yard or a factory, you do not even need to model the main line. Yards and factories could be situated away from the main line, sometimes even a mile or two away on their own short branch line. Therefore, the exit from the fiddle yard can represent the short line that connects to the main line – all you need to model is the yard itself.

The goods yard can be as large or as small as you want it, from a single siding to a huge hump-fed marshalling yard. The latter would make for a fascinating room-sized project in OO gauge or N gauge. If space is at a premium, remember that one siding often serves multiple purposes, which is great news if you like shunting puzzles. Consider a siding with a goods shed and a cattle dock. You will need to remove the wagons from one to access the other – a headache for the real shunter, but a challenge for you. Many goods yards are cramped and difficult places to operate, especially in urban areas. This

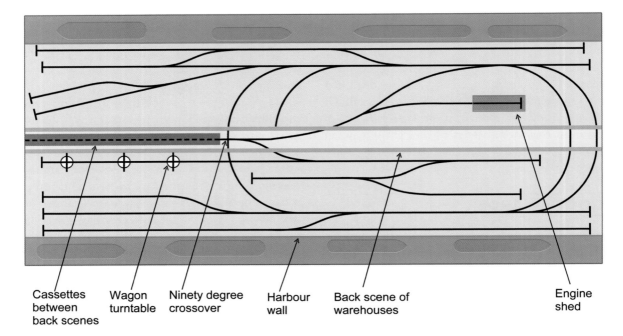

Cassettes between back scenes   Wagon turntable   Ninety degree crossover   Harbour wall   Back scene of warehouses   Engine shed

This dockyard plan is a variation on the theme of a back-to-back layout with interchangeable cassettes between the central back scenes. The tight radii used in dockyards allow for a loop from one side to the other, so you can watch the trains go round as well as having lots of shunting. The two half-circles at the right-hand side form a reasonable run-round loop. The layout could be narrowed by omitting the outer tracks on each side that run along the harbour wall.

can only be good news for modellers who want an interesting layout in a small space.

DOCKYARDS

Railways have been an integral part of dockyards and ports from the very beginning. From the earliest days of stevedores manhandling all manner of goods, to the massive modern container ports, the dockyard has been an essential trans-shipment point for international and even coastal goods. Like railways, dockyards can be big places and many of them had their own internal railway systems and perhaps their own locomotives. Many railway companies owned ports and used their own locomotives.

A useful feature of many dockyards, at least for the modeller, was the use of very tight radii in the track. Despite the vast amounts of space that dock-

yards can occupy, there was often a need to go round tight corners and buildings, which must have led to a lot of squealing of flanges. Think about some of the classic dockyard shunting locomotives like the USA 0-6-0T – they all had a very short wheelbase to cope with the very sharp corners. You really can justify the tightest track radius.

Modelling a part of a dock or port offers plenty of operating potential. They would have been incredibly busy places, with ships being loaded and unloaded as quickly as possible, sometimes in an effort to beat the tides. The shunting of wagons must have been brisk, to say the least. All manner of goods would have passed both ways through the ports, much of it in bulk requiring many of the same wagon type, such as for iron ore, sand, timber and, of course, coal. Where once we sent our coal out through the ports to power the world, we now bring it in through the ports to feed our power stations.

Ashley Toone's OO gauge layout 'Windmill Road' occupies just 72in by 14in (1.83m by 0.36m) including fiddle yard, yet it brilliantly conveys the atmosphere of a bustling modern-era wagon repair yard. As many of the wagons are for engineering, this could just as easily be a permanent way yard. (Photo by Steve Flint courtesy of Peco Publications and Publicity Ltd)

A lot of railway modellers are also ship modellers as well. What better way to combine two rewarding and constructive hobbies than to build a dockyard layout and get the best of both worlds?

WAGON REPAIR YARDS

Just as motive power depots are required for the maintenance and repair of locomotives, so too is somewhere for wagon repair. This design is a variation on the goods yard; in fact, many simple wagon repairs were carried out in situ in a goods yard. More involved repairs or rebuilds would be carried out at a dedicated wagon repair yard. The large steam-era railway companies largely built their own wagons at their own major works; however, there were millions of privately owned wagons, mostly shuttling

coal from colliery to merchant, which required a substantial business in the manufacture and repair of wagons. Even on the modern railway, there is a small number of wagon repair companies with their own private sidings.

A design for a wagon repair yard layout falls somewhere between a goods yard and a factory. There would be sidings to store new wagons waiting to be collected and wagons coming in for repair. Many modellers like to keep their models as clean as the day they were built, which is not really accurate as brake and coal dust soon made wagons dirty, so the lines of new wagons straight from the paint shop are a case of a 'prototype for everything'. There would be wagons bringing in timber, iron and steel, plus coal to fuel the steam-powered machinery.

Like a factory or locomotive shed, you do not need to model the entirety of the wagon shop, just enough to give the essence of what it is. A siding can enter the workshop and pass through to another small fiddle yard, perhaps using cassettes; that allows more rolling stock to flow through the layout than would otherwise be possible.

PERMANENT WAY YARDS

If you love wagons covering a broad period of designs, you can do no better than to model a permanent way yard, otherwise known as the engineers' department. A lot of revenue-earning stock drifted into the engineers' fleet towards the end of its useful life, rubbing shoulders alongside purpose-built wagons, to give the most eclectic mix of rolling stock you will ever find in one place. Permanent way yards are often in the middle of nowhere – their customer is the railway itself, so there is no need to be near to other industry or a station. They can be quite rural, which means you can consider using a lot of trees as a back scene, maybe even a few small hills, or a road leading down from a road overbridge that masks the entrance to the fiddle yard.

This is another variation of the goods yard and falls somewhere between that and a wagon repair yard. A permanent way yard will generally have very little infrastructure, maybe just a few cranes to load and unload track parts, some kind of accommodation or office for staff and sidings to store the engineering wagons. This minimalist approach to infrastructure can work well for the railway modeller, as it is then just a case of thinking about laying track. For operation, engineering trains need to be formed as required for the job in hand (ballast, track, or a mixture of both). This preparation of a train can be just like the shunting puzzle of 'Inglenook Sidings'.

PRESERVED RAILWAYS

Modelling the many preserved railways of the United Kingdom is not as popular as you might think. Such railways run an eclectic selection of rolling stock based on what is to hand, or what is on loan and visiting from another railway. You really can run everything from steam to diesel without someone telling you that they never ran together like that in real life. Most preserved railways occupy the former premises of a long-gone railway, either taking over the goods yard or former motive power depot. Some are lucky enough to have sizable infrastructure left behind, while others have to make do with a much smaller site.

Things can get very cramped on these small sites, which need to serve the multiple purposes of locomotive and carriage maintenance, and often wagons for the permanent way department as well. This is great news for the modeller with limited space, as here is a design for a model railway layout that has steam and diesel locomotives and a few items of rolling stock, all packed into a small space. Like the real preserved railway, you may even have room for a small platform to carry out brake van rides. Not all the sidings may necessarily be connected; many preserved sites put some track down to store the long-term restoration projects until their time comes. This would allow you to make a background of rolling stock that 'goes nowhere' at the rear of the layout.

CHAPTER NINE

MICRO-LAYOUTS

The word 'micro' is one of those that embodies the late twentieth century – when there is nothing left to invent, simply make the existing inventions smaller. For railway modellers, it is not a case of trying to make the smallest possible layout (though for novelty layout builders, this is where the fun lies). It is more a case of taking the space available (no matter how small) and attempting to portray convincingly a railway scene within that space. Many model railway layout builders class their layout as a 'micro-layout', yet it is actually a hard thing to define clearly, since there are so many factors beyond the obvious fact that the layout is small. Micro-layouts tend to focus on just one railway scene (such as a motive power depot), rather than the entirety of even a modest station, so perhaps more than anything they are a microcosm.

THE DEFINITION OF A MICRO-LAYOUT

A micro-layout is, by definition, a very small layout indeed. There is no clear definition of just how small a layout has to be before it is classed as a micro-layout. Nor are there guidelines and rules that define a micro-layout. Obviously, if you build a layout in a box file, that is clearly a micro-layout. The problem with trying to find a definition is not so much how small a micro-layout is, but, rather, how big does it have to be before it is no longer a micro-layout? There are some common attributes that make a classic micro-layout, so the following will outline what you might expect to see in one.

Layout types such as the fold-up layout and ironing-board layout are all portable – so that's the first thing about a micro-layout. You could literally take it off a shelf or out of a box, put it on the table, plug in and away you go. This portability means that it is lightweight, easily transportable, yet durable in its construction. An ironing-board layout is probably limited to about 4ft (1.2m) in length and

no more than 18in (0.45m) wide. A fold-up layout could be these dimensions, but twice over, literally folded over on itself. The more robust construction required for the hinges might make it on the heavy side for truly easy portability.

The next clue to categorizing a micro-layout is the minimalist amount of railway that is usually included. If you are working in a tightly defined space, there is only room for maybe one or two turnouts and perhaps a few sidings. This is where you really are working hard with the design principles outlined in this book in order to portray a railway scene realistically in miniature. You will probably only have a few buildings, which are likely to be in low relief against the back scene. You do not even need to have any turnouts on the layout – a micro-layout can be designed with a couple of sidings that are fed by a traverser or cassettes from off-stage.

Some modellers feel that a micro-layout is so minimalist that it is little more than a diorama. In other branches of modelling, such as military modelling, dioramas are popular, but they are less so in railway modelling. Some modellers build dioramas that can later be incorporated into a larger layout, while others use them as a photographic setting for rolling stock. A diorama is static by definition, so perhaps a micro-layout could be described as a 'working diorama'.

The chosen scale also has a bearing on what defines a micro-layout. Even a single turnout and a siding for a few wagons will require quite a length in O gauge. This would need one, maybe even two baseboards – hardly a tiny portable layout in terms of baseboard infrastructure, yet still a micro-layout in terms of the minimalist approach to what is actually included.

Oval layouts are certainly outside the scope of micro-layouts, unless they are Z gauge in a coffee table. This means that you will need a fiddle yard of some kind. A very important part of defining the

Small end-to-end layouts, particularly micro-layouts, do not have enough track for the running in of new locomotives. This is a Gaugemaster rolling road, whose adjustable rollers allow any locomotive from a steam engine to a bogie locomotive to be accommodated. This particular rolling road can also be used as an ordinary controller for the layout itself.

credibility of a micro-layout is the means of transitioning the layout to the fiddle yard. The classic device is the overbridge, carrying a road or another railway line. This is a perfect solution, as you can have as many tracks as you want under the bridge and, by making the bridge deep enough, the entry to the fiddle yard is disguised.

ROLLING ROADS

Any end-to-end layout inevitably means a short run from starting in the fiddle yard to terminating in the station. Even on a big layout, this may take less than half a minute. On a micro-layout, the journey can be measured in seconds. It is similar to driving your car to the corner shop; the engine has not even warmed up by the time you get there. While electric model railway locomotives do not really need to warm up (although a warmed-up electric motor can perform differently), one feature of the new generation of locomotives is the need to run them in for a couple

of hours in each direction. With older locomotives, it helps to run them for a while after maintenance, especially if a little bit of lubrication has been applied.

As layouts without a continuous loop do not allow for continuous running, consider investing in a 'rolling road'. These come in various designs, from dedicated rolling roads for workshops to more adaptable systems that sit on the layout's track and thus take their power from the track. What they all have in common is a set of rollers for the locomotive wheels that are adjustable to the wheelbase and the number of wheels. These rollers provide power to the locomotive and thus allow you to have as much continuous running as you need – without actually going anywhere.

ADVANTAGES OF MICRO-LAYOUTS

If you are a relative newcomer to model railways, building a micro-layout has two significant advantages. First, its relative simplicity means that you won't be overwhelmed by taking on a project that is too big, with the worst possible outcome, that you become disheartened and lose interest. A 'quick' layout will bring quick results. Second, in the unlikely event that one aspect does not quite go according to plan, you will not have wasted too much money, time and effort. You can consider scrapping the layout and starting again in the sure knowledge that the next one will be better, as you will have learned so much from the first one.

Like a magician, a micro-layout can use a lot of tricks to deceive the eye into thinking that the railway is bigger than it really is. There is one final thing that defines a micro-layout, or, rather, it defines the builder of the layout – ingenuity. Modellers come up with the most ingenious solutions to build utterly convincing layouts in the smallest of spaces. A micro-layout may be a small layout, but it always reflects a big imagination.

TYPES OF MICRO-LAYOUTS

Almost without exception, you will find that micro-layouts are some kind of terminus. They may be a terminus station, yet they can also be a goods yard, or a motive power depot. It is easy to feed the trains in from just one side. Some railway subjects do not lend themselves to the micro-layout format. Anything in the landscape, be it rural or urban, or a four-track main line, just will not work in a micro-layout. The terminus qualities of goods yards and motive power depots make them ideal for micro-layouts and the cramped location can be prototypical, which means that the layout will still look realistic.

STATIONS

Can a micro-layout contain a whole station? The answer is yes, certainly in N gauge, as you can incorporate a platform, run-round loop and a few sidings in a very small space indeed. There are several tricks to make a station seem bigger, or to use a larger scale within the same baseboard space.

First, remember that it is not necessary to model the whole station. There are plenty of real-life examples where a good proportion of the station is hidden under a canopy or a bridge. Just the very ends of the platforms may stick out. One then imagines that the rest of the platforms continue out of sight, say, beyond the bridge that acts as the view blocker to the fiddle yard. In actual fact, the platforms are very short and do not continue into the fiddle yard. You only need to have enough platform for one engine and one or two coaches – imagination says that the remaining five coaches of the train are on the other side of the bridge. You can still run

'Rosneath' in N gauge by Peter Johnson is small enough to fit on an ironing board, yet it contains a station, run-round loop and three sidings. Note the turnout at the extreme right by the overbridge, where the layout enters the fiddle yard so that it forms part of the layout's headshunt and run-round loop. The dual function of the track beyond the bridge as fiddle yard and headshunt means a saving in space compared to having them as separate pieces of track.

The Great Western Railway was one of the first companies to remove the cost of maintaining a run-round loop by introducing the 'auto-coach' (a single coach with a small loco at one end). The concept of a motorized coach became the DMU. Although DMUs have got longer, they are still a short passenger train that does not require a run-round loop – perfect for a micro-layout.

round the 'train' consisting of one coach and draw it out of the 'station'. The more modern prototype railway operations catered for by two-car DMUs are ideal for this kind of charade.

A traverser or cassettes can be used to represent the other end of a station run-round loop. The same mechanism can also feed a siding, or maybe a turnout to two sidings at the front or the rear of the layout so as to allow some shunting operations on that layout. You will be amazed at how easy it is with a little imagination and a few simple tricks to represent a modestly busy station in even the smallest of spaces that make up a micro-layout.

GOODS YARDS

The goods yard is one of the classic micro-layout situations. Most real goods yards were quite large, but it is their sheer variety that is the inspiration for many micro-layouts. The goods yard literally comes in all shapes and sizes, from just a single siding poking out from under a bridge to serve a coal merchant, to larger concerns with many turnouts and sidings, several coal merchants and even more than one goods shed. Urban goods yards could be squeezed in-between existing buildings with not much room to spare, so, for once, you are quite at liberty to cram things in yet still be realistic. As with the station, the fiddle yard offers a few tricks. You can save the length required for some of the turnouts by using a traverser or cassettes. On the layout, a three-way

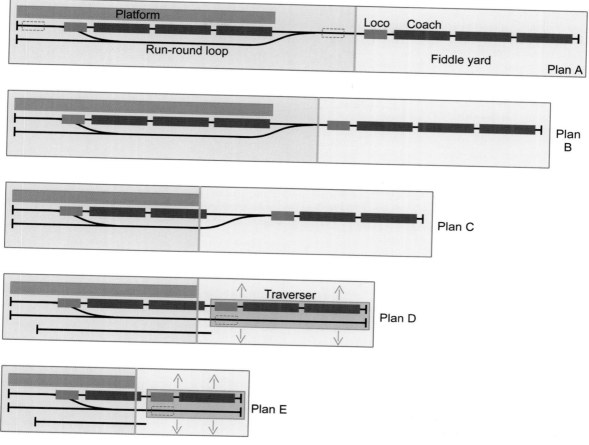

Platform

Run-round loop

Loco   Coach

Fiddle yard

Plan A

Plan B

Plan C

Traverser

Plan D

Plan E

This is a series of plans showing the transition from a small layout to a micro-layout. Plan A is a basic terminus station with a run-round loop capable of taking three coaches. The dotted outlines of the locomotive show the space needed for it to run round. The fiddle yard has to be big enough to take the locomotive and three coaches. Plan B is only fractionally smaller, as the space for the loco to run round by the scenic break (such as an overbridge) has been moved into the fiddle yard since it will be empty when the train is in the station. Plan C is more radical, in that the scenic break cuts a section off the station. Now, only two coaches are required and both the scenic layout and the fiddle yard can be shortened accordingly. The turnout in the fiddle yard for the run-round still takes up space, so in Plan D this has been removed by using a traverser. Additionally, the traverser now allows access to a goods siding at the front of the layout. With Plan E, we arrive at a micro-layout by removing a second coach from the train. This layout is now less than half the length of the original design, yet it still allows the same basic operations to be carried out.

point is a huge space-saver and totally prototypical in this situation.

Although most micro-layouts only put a fiddle yard at one side, with a goods yard you can run into a goods shed at the rear of the layout and carry the line outwards on a single-track fiddle yard that is easily attached when the layout is set up (either on a table, or supported by a simple leg if the layout is free-standing). This allows more stock to be brought on to and through the layout, then out the other side. The goods yard building is a perfect view blocker and, like the magician's hat, it will swallow more wagons than the eye tells you it should.

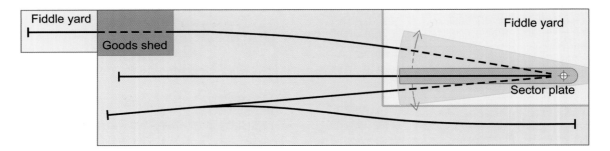

This is a typical micro-layout plan for a small goods yard or industrial facility. Using a single-track sector plate in the fiddle yard saves a lot of room that would be taken up by turnouts and allows the track to enter the layout at a series of angles for variety. There is a kickback siding at the front, which could return to the fiddle yard, or, as here, run in front of it. The rear track runs into a building such as a goods shed and carries through into a small single-track add-on fiddle yard; by swapping wagons on and off, the building can hold more wagons than would otherwise be possible.

MOTIVE POWER DEPOTS

This is a very popular type of micro-layout indeed, and probably accounts for half the micro-layouts that you will see. It is ideal for those of us with large collections of locomotives, as it provides somewhere to display them, yet not in a static kind of way. You can also justify that big express locomotive that you would not otherwise be able to get on to such a small layout.

The motive power depot layout is just as suitable to the steam era or the modern diesel era as they still serve the same function. Locomotives basically need to be serviced, repaired, fuelled and stored, and most sites will move the locomotives around from one function to another. The slightly more inefficient steam era is a little more intense with ash disposal, watering and even turning (if you can fit a turntable into the design), as well as fuelling. You

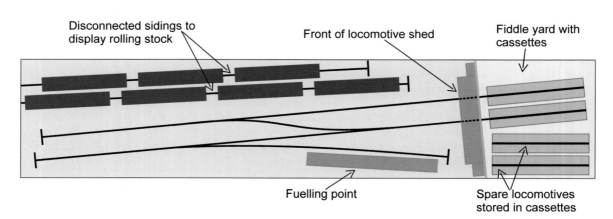

This is an idea for a modern-era motive power depot micro-layout. The fiddle yard is very small, enough to accommodate one locomotive in a cassette with space to store locomotives in spare cassettes. Just the front of the shed is modelled, with locomotives emerging to visit the fuelling point at the front, or to return to the shed. There are two disconnected sidings at the rear that can be used to display other rolling stock, such as coaches or a breakdown crane. Note also how everything is set at a slight angle to avoid emphasizing the obviously rectangular shape of the small baseboard.

can even bring a few wagons on to the layout, as fuel needs to be brought in (coal in open wagons, traction gas oil in tankers), as well as spare parts (in the so-called 'enparts' vans, which were usually a wonderfully eclectic collection of former revenue-earning wagons and even coaching stock).

Do not forget that perennial favourite of the motive power depot – the breakdown crane. This is a fairly big piece of railway machinery. However, you do not actually have to connect the track on which it is stored to the fiddle yard or the other track on the layout. It can be a display-only track at the front or rear. Snow ploughs are often found spending their summer holidays in motive power depots, so the same trick can be used for these. You can even put a couple of rows of tracks with coaching stock at the rear of the layout to make it seem busier than it would otherwise be.

As with the goods shed in the goods yard, you can take a number of the tracks in a motive power depot into the locomotive shed itself if you include that in the design. The shed can be open at the rear; real locomotive sheds are long and wide, yet only a portion of the shed in one corner needs to be modelled. In the shed, you could use simple short cassettes to swap locomotives, giving the impression that the shed is swallowing dozens of locomotives. The shed could even be made into the fiddle yard, with locomotives entering the layout by coming out of the shed to use the turntable, coaling stage, fuelling point and so on.

NOVELTY LAYOUTS

The modellers who build what is referred to here as 'novelty' layouts may well disagree with the term. After all, a layout, no matter how small, or how unusual, is something that brings pleasure to its creator. These 'extreme' micro-layouts are quite a challenge to produce, so it is possibly unfair to dismiss them as mere novelty, and certainly they are not trivial. This section takes a look at modelling in the ultimate of small spaces. The inspiration to be gained is simple – if someone can build a layout in a shoebox, then no matter how small a space you may

think you have, there's always some kind of layout that can be put into it.

SUITCASES

At first glance, building a layout in a good old-fashioned type of suitcase is anything but a novelty, since they are the ultimate in solid portability and storage. Any kind of suitcase or musical instrument case offers a ready-made solid box to support the layout – all you have to do is open the lid, plug in the power, put some rolling stock on the rails and away you go.

You might be able to manage a couple of sidings and some shunting with OO gauge in a suitcase, but really it is going to require the smaller scales of N gauge and below to make the most of it. Working inside a suitcase (in a manner of speaking) is going to be tricky. The best advice is to cut a piece of plywood to the shape of the inside of the suitcase so that you can work on your layout with good all-round access and simply drop it into the suitcase when it is finished.

BOX FILES

There seems to be almost a subculture of micro-layout building that involves nothing more than a box file. If you challenge anyone to attempt the impossible, they will likely take you up on it. Railway modellers love a challenge; problem-solving seems to be part of our make-up and how often do you hear that something was attempted 'just to see if it could be done'. Like the suitcase, using box files is not as odd as it first seems, since they are very sturdily built in order to store a fair weight of paper. Flip up the lid and away you go. Once you have finished your operating session, the box file just stores away on a shelf.

A good quality box file will store your miniature layout safely. The lid will keep the dust out. All the work is done for you – just add a model railway. You might consider cutting a hole in one end to allow access to a fiddle yard of sorts (usually just a piece of track) and this is perfectly allowable within the 'rules' of box-file layouts.

ABOVE: 'Furth DB Museum' is an N gauge layout by Kevin Player that has been built into an old guitar case. This is wide enough to allow a half circle of track at the left-hand side, with plenty of room inside for a motive power depot, including a locomotive shed and turntable. Note the clever use of a sky and building back scene inside the lid.

BELOW: This is a basic mock-up inside a standard box file using N gauge set track components from a Peco track pack and a few items of rolling stock of differing sizes for perspective. Placing the track at an angle makes it fractionally longer and avoids an obvious parallelism with the walls of the box file. It would be a simple matter to drill some holes in the side to allow the track to join to either a simple fiddle yard or to another box file.

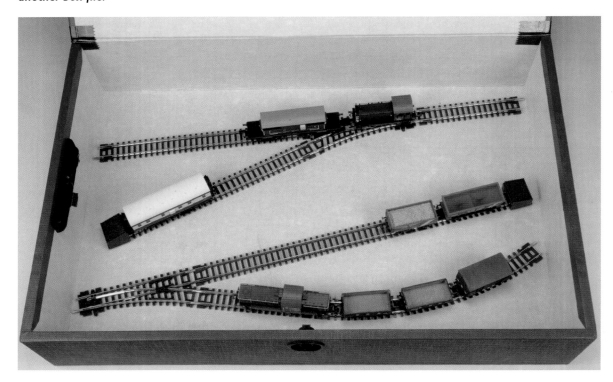

Why stop at one box file? Modular layouts are usually much bigger, but the concept is a set of linked scenes made by different modellers that come together to make a whole. So why not a series of box files linked together? You could easily get three box files on to an ironing board, even more on the dining table. Like modular layouts, by rigidly defining where the track goes at the ends, the order in which the box files are joined together could be changed. Imagine being able to choose, before an operating session, whether to put the station before the goods yard, or maybe the factory section?

Box-file layouts prove that a constrained space is no barrier to building some kind of model railway layout. Sometimes, you just have to 'think outside of the box'.

INDEX